God's Most Precious Jewels are Crystallized Tears

Other Books by Barbara Johnson

Where Does a Mother Go to Resign?

Fresh Elastic for Stretched-Out Moms

Stick a Geranium in Your Hat and Be Happy!

Splashes of Joy in the Cesspools of Life

*Pack Up Your Gloomees in a Great Big Box,
Then Sit on the Lid and Laugh!*

Mama, Get the Hammer! There's a Fly on Papa's Head!

I'm So Glad You Told Me What I Didn't Wanna Hear

Living Somewhere Between Estrogen and Death

Boomerang Joy

He's Gonna Toot, and I'm Gonna Scoot!

Leaking Laughs Between Pampers and Depends

Children's Books

The Upside-Down Frown and Splashes of Joy

Super-Scrumptious Jelly Donuts Sprinkled with Hugs

The Tasty Taffy Tale and Super-Stretching the Truth

The Pepperoni Parade and the Power of Prayer

BARBARA JOHNSON

God's Most Precious Jewels are Crystallized Tears

W PUBLISHING GROUP™

www.wpublishinggroup.com

A Division of Thomas Nelson, Inc.
www.ThomasNelson.com

Published by W Publishing Group, a Division of Thomas Nelson, Inc., P.O. Box 141000, Nashville, Tennessee 37214.

Unless otherwise indicated, Scripture quotations used in this book are from the Holy Bible, New International Version (NIV). Copyright © 1973, 1978, 1984 International Bible Society. Used by permission of Zondervan Bible Publishers. Other Scripture references are from the following sources:

The King James Version of the Bible (KJV).

The Living Bible (TLB), copyright © 1971 by Tyndale House Publishers, Wheaton, Illinois. Used by permission.

New Century Version (NCV) © 1987, 1988, 1991 by W Publishing Group, Nashville, Tennessee 37214. Used by permission.

The New King James Version (NKJV), copyright © 1979, 1980, 1982, 1992, Thomas Nelson, Inc., Publisher.

The Message (MSG). Copyright © by Eugene H. Peterson 1993, 1994, 1995. Used by permission of NavPress Publishng Group.

The twelve women's stories in this volume are true. However, in some instances names and specific details have been changed to protect identities. The chapter-ending collections of quips and jokes have been contributed by the author's many friends, and we have diligently tried to identify the material's origin. Where no source is named, the writer is unknown, and the author claims no rights or ownership.

Library of Congress Cataloging-in-Publication Data
Johnson, Barbara (Barbara E.)
    God's most precious jewels are crystallized tears / Barbara Johnson.
      p. cm.
    ISBN 0-8499-3779-5
    1. Christian women—United States—Biography. 2. Christian biography—United States. I. Title.

BR1713 .J64 2001
248.8'43—dc21

2001017606

Printed in the United States of America

01 02 03 04 05 PHX 8 7 6 5 4

Contents

Opening the Jewel Box   vii

1. A Hostess in God's Filling Station   1

2. A Broken Heart Held Together with Laughter   17

3. Sharing the Wealth of God's Unconditional Love   33

4. Laughter Bubblin' Up from the Boiler Room   47

5. A Quiet Missionary in Our Midst   59

6. Unspeakable Sorrow . . . Inexhaustible Faith . . .
   and a Crazy Craving for Laughter   73

7. Using That Spiritual Get-Out-of-Guilt-Free Card   87

8. Waiting for Another Chance to Say,
   "I Love You"   105

9. At the End, a New Beginning   121

10. Reaching Out from Death's Doorway   133

11. From the Pieces of a Broken Life . . . a Stained-
    Glass Window of God's Beautiful Love   147

12. I Never Knew You Lived So Close to the Floor   159

Like the Stars of the Morning   173

Acknowledgments   175

Notes   177

Opening the Jewel Box

mrs. Provencher, an old lady who loved cats, lived next door to me for many years. She was a sweet neighbor with no family except her swarm of wild cats, and I tried to look out for her, even though I'm definitely *not* a cat lover.

As she advanced in age, she got too feeble to lug in the heavy bags of catfood and Kitty Litter, so I dutifully bought the items at the grocery store for her, struggled to lift them into my car, hauled them home, then strained my back carrying them to her door. The cats—there must have been fifty of them—were everywhere: indoors, outdoors, all over the place. Many times I saw them digging in her garden, making a bathroom in the rows of chard. Then she would call my house and say she'd made some chard soup for us to enjoy! Barney was usually the one who would run next door to pick it up and, just to get my goat, he would always rave that we LOVED that chard soup so Mrs. Provencher would keep making it for us. The fact was, as soon as he brought it home, I dumped it down the sink! I wasn't about to eat soup made from chard that grew in the cats' outhouse! Then she would call and ask how we liked it, and I'd thank her and assure her, "That soup doesn't last long over here!"

Well, to be truthful, it was not exactly fun living next door to that sweet old cat lover. Not only did my back ache from carrying Kitty Litter, but the swarming cats and the chard soup just about did me in.

Then she died. And within a few months came the most extraordinary news: Mrs. Provencher had had no children, and she had bequeathed to me her fabulous diamond rings! Now, whenever those sparkling diamonds on my fingers catch my eye, I think of her gracious goodness and how my negative ordeal became a bountiful blessing. I remember how appreciated I felt and how needed, and I don't think of the backaches, the annoying cats, or the chard soup. (Well, maybe a little. But I remember it with laughter. And Bill tells me, "You earned every sparkle on those diamonds for caring for those cats.")

Hard times *can* bring a sparkle to our lives—and to the lives of others. This book is a collection of true stories about trials and ordeals that crystallized into blessings. It's about women who have persevered through extraordinary circumstances— much more difficult situations than enduring cats and hauling catfood. And today their tears have crystallized into jewels of courage and comfort for many, many others.

These are women whose lives have touched mine in some way, and through that encounter we have both been changed. Most of these ladies are not well known. Most are ordinary women who hold jobs, tend to families, or brag about their grandchildren, just as you may do. The primary facts of their stories, as amazing as they may seem, are accurate. But in some cases their names and certain details have been changed to protect the identities of the women and their loved ones.

These gals could have let their past hurts consume them— as many grieving women do today. Instead, they reach out to those around them, sharing love, spreading encouragement, lending a helping hand to those in need. They are gems, these women. In God's wondrous way, their tears have crystallized into blessings of hope, and they have become precious jewels to those persons, known and unknown, whose lives they've touched.

Even if all of them *could* let their identities be known, I think it's best that we use some pseudonyms. That way you may wonder, when you stand in line at the grocery store or settle into a pew at church or make a new friend at a meeting somewhere, if the woman next to you is *that* woman you read about—the one whose amazing story so inspired you. These women are out there today, living among you. They are heroes of the faith, and I'm honored to know them.

When one of my friends heard about my latest writing endeavor, she sent me a book entitled *Bible Jewels*. Published in 1867, the little book's cover is falling off, and the pages are brittle and stained. But the message contained within those pages is as encouraging today as it was when it was written more than a century ago. It begins with God's promise for those who "feared the LORD, and that thought upon his name," the promise given in Malachi 3:16–17 (KJV): "They shall be mine, saith the LORD of hosts, in that day when I make up my jewels."

In Isaiah 62:2–3, God said, "You will have a new name, which the LORD himself will give you. You will be like a beautiful crown in the LORD's hand, like a king's crown in your God's hand" (NCV).

Imagine! We are jewels in the Lord's crown. The little book says we're like jewels in three ways:

• *We're beautiful.* God made us, and as the T-shirt says, "God don't make no junk!" But like jewels, we have no real beauty of our own, no power to sparkle and shine until we stand in the light. And you know who the Light is, don't you? It's Jesus! The Bible says, "But unto you that fear my name shall the Sun of righteousness arise with healing in his wings" (Malachi 4:2, KJV). Jesus "gives light to his people, just as the sun gives light to the world. . . . And the stronger the light is that falls on a jewel, the more beautiful it appears. . . . The nearer we get to Jesus, the more we know of him and love him, the more beautiful we shall become."[1]

• *We're valuable.* Here's how the little book puts it: "The soul of the youngest child is worth more than all the gold and silver, and all the diamonds and rubies, and gems and jewels in the world. Jesus said that if a man should gain the whole world but lose his soul by it, he would make a very bad bargain. Jesus knows what the soul is worth, for he *made* it. And when it was lost he paid the price that was required to redeem it. . . . That price was his own precious blood."[2]

And the third reason Christians are like jewels is the focus of *this* book. You see, like jewels, Christians are . . .

• . . . *hard to polish!* Every gemstone must be polished before it can be placed in the setting. Just as a jeweler uses diamond-edged tools and files to turn a rough stone into a beautiful gem, the trials that roll through our lives, fracturing our hearts and grinding us down, serve to polish us so that we shine more brilliantly as God's most precious jewels.

And now, there's one more thing to mention before we get started . . .

Those of you who have read my books know that I just can't let things get too heavy. And the stories you'll read here have the potential to leave you blubbering on the kitchen floor. So, as usual, I've sprinkled a few gems of silliness and encouragement throughout these pages—jokes and cartoons and heart-touching stories my friends have sent me from all the corners of the earth. I've also added to each chapter some tidbits about gemstones themselves that intrigued me. As always, where no source is given, the authors of these little quips and quotes are unknown to me. But I'm pleased to share their words of mirth and wisdom with you, hoping they will help you laugh through *your* tears. Remember: As soap is to the body, tears are to the soul.

Joyfully!

Barb

P.S. If you would like to write to the women whose stories are shared in this book, they would be happy to hear from you. On the envelope, be sure to specify which "jewel" you're writing to. The publisher will make sure your message is forwarded to the appropriate woman. Send your letter to:

God's Most Precious Jewels
(Lynda or Rose or Evelyn or Maggie, etc.)
c/o W Publishing Group
P.O. Box 141000
Nashville, TN 37214

Jewels

When He cometh, when He cometh,
To make up His jewels.
All His jewels, precious jewels,
His loved and His own.

Like the stars of the morning
His bright crown adorning,
They shall shine in their beauty,
Bright gems for His own.

—WILLIAM O. CUSHING, 1823–1902,
AND GEORGE F. ROOT, 1820–1895

A Hostess in God's Filling Station

Joanne's gem: *I have sought counseling and help here and there. But . . . what's helped the most [has been] just running—running—to God in His Word and basking in His presence. . . . "Joy is not in the absence of suffering but in the presence of God."*

the little teardrop of love that later crystallized into Spatula Ministries first sparkled in June 1973 at a gas station in Alaska. Since then, there have been lots of *real* tears, *wet* tears. But from those tears, blessings have flowed. I hope this story crystallizes into a gem of encouragement for you.

Many readers know the story of how our son Tim and a friend had driven Tim's little Volkswagen Beetle to Alaska on a lark, planning to see the forty-ninth state and have an adventure or two. Now I'm delighted to tell the *rest* of the story—Joanne McReynolds's story—even though it is bittersweet.

On one of their first days in Alaska, the boys pulled into a gas station for a fill-up. Working at the gas station that summer day was a former pastor named Ted McReynolds. After serving ministries around the country with fantastic zeal and leading many believers to the Lord with his enthusiastic manner, Ted had left the ministry because of some personal problems. But he still had a heart full of passion for sharing Christ with others, and he was unbelievably gifted as a soul winner. That part of his ministry never changed, even after he worshiped from the pew rather than the pulpit. When Tim showed up at that gas station, Ted was a schoolteacher, working at the station during the summer to support his wife, Joanne, and their two children, Danny, five, and Pammy, four.

There's no way to know what Ted actually said to the boys that day. He might have commented on the bumper sticker that said, "Alaska or Bust." But we do know that before the Volkswagen's tank was filled and the windshield was washed, he had invited them to a Bible study in his home and to a home-cooked meal prepared by Joanne.

The boys, tired and dusty, gratefully accepted the invitation and arrived at Ted and Joanne's home that evening to join some other young people who had come for the meal and the Bible study. "We were always having things going on at our house," Joanne recalled. "I think the young people felt enveloped by the love they felt among us. There's just something hearty and substantial about people who go to Alaska."

Joanne didn't always know who would appear at her dinner table—and she never really minded. She and Ted and their two children enjoyed welcoming guests into their home. She had a routine that made guests feel like part of the family, and knowing Tim, that routine was as strong a magnet as were Ted's fervent discussions of the Scriptures. All these years later, I marvel at her simple but endearing graciousness and the ease with which she served a houseful of dinner guests. She truly had the gift of hospitality.

"I loved to make all the preparations ahead of time so I could sit down and enjoy the meal and the people and not be running back and forth to the kitchen," she said. "Most of the time the meal would revolve around a large main dish like chicken divan or lasagna. I made a habit of having every-thing—including the water pitcher for refills—on the table or on a serving table so nobody had to get up. It was important to Ted and me, even on a daily basis when we didn't have guests, that the table was attractive and settings were correctly placed. When we gathered at the table, the plates would be stacked in front of Ted, and he would serve the food—fill the plates and pass them down the table. That was just the way we did it. Then we all ate and talked and laughed together. And when we were finished, I would get the coffee and dessert ready while Ted cleared the dishes and got them ready for the dishwasher."

Serving Up the Gospel

It was a ritual Ted and Joanne repeated hundreds of times wherever they lived—in five different states as well as in the Alaskan bush, where they taught school in an isolated community accessible only by plane. They didn't just preach the gospel; they *literally* shared it by the way they opened their home to others.

"We were always wrapped up in people, and our home was open," Joanne said. "Usually we had someone living with us. Our kids, Dan and Pam, both had trundle beds, and sometimes they woke up in the morning and might not know who was sleeping in the 'trundle.'"

Dan and Pam surely got to know Tim and his friend, how-ever. They stayed connected with the McReynoldses two months, sleeping and working out of the nearby home of the McReynoldses' friends who were out of state at that time. Tim rededicated his life to the Lord while he was there, and his friend became a Christian. Tim was bubbling over with enthusiasm when he called me on August 1 and asked what I was doing to celebrate the first of the month—one of my little traditions. I told him, "I was just waiting for a collect call from *you!*"

Tim said he was coming home. "Mom," he told me, "I've got a spring in my step and a sparkle in my eye. I'm on fire for the Lord, and I can't wait to get home in five days and tell you about it."

Tim and his friend said good-bye to Ted and Joanne and the church friends they had come to love. Then they piled into the little Volkswagen and headed south. Only a few hours later, at one hour after midnight, a two-ton truck with a drunk driver behind the wheel plowed into the little car, and both boys were immediately ushered into the presence of God.

Ted and Joanne flew down to California for the memorial service, and Ted delivered an unforgettable message to the hundreds of friends and family members who gathered that day. Even now, twenty years later, listening to Ted's inspiring words on that tape brings me comfort.

I love the way Joanne describes Ted's charisma: "He simply used what he had, wherever he was. He was tireless and absolutely fearless. He was just so confident that those whom God had made ready to hear and had placed in his path would receive Christ if they just had a proper presentation. Ted led hundreds of people to the Lord. He had a super personality. He was friendly but very direct. Still, he shared the message in such a clear and winsome way that people wanted to listen. And, not willing to leave a 'new babe' hanging, wherever possible he personally bought them a Bible then taught them or took them to church."

Five years earlier, another of our four sons, Steven, had been killed in Vietnam. Soon, Bill and I started reaching out to other parents of Vietnam victims, calling them to share their grief and remind them of God's comforting love. When we met Ted and Joanne, we were inspired by their zealous yet easygoing ministry—so warm and comforting yet so passionate. We decided to step up our own work with other hurting parents. We wanted to serve the Lord with the same compassion they had shared with so many.

Since then, to the best of our abilities and in our own humble way, that's what we've done. In those years we've touched a lot of lives. And some of those heartbroken parents we've worked with have caught from us the spark of Jesus' love and servanthood that we learned from Ted and Joanne. And the tears of those grief-stricken parents have crystallized into gems of blessing to others. Some of their stories fill the remainder of this book.

Tears of Grief, Gems of Blessing

A year after Tim's death, we learned that Larry, our third son, was a homosexual, and our lives were once again thrown into chaos. After I argued with Larry, saying all the wrong things (including the statement that he *couldn't* be homosexual because he was a Christian), he fled from our home. He disowned us, changed his name, and said he never wanted to see us again. Then he disappeared for eleven years in the homosexual lifestyle. In our grief, we once again reached out to Ted and Joanne for solace—and for inspiration. Ted was able to give us this help because of his own personal struggles in this area. Soon our efforts to help other hurting parents widened to include Christian parents who were struggling to cope with their adult children's homosexuality. It was during that time that our ministry finally took on a name: Spatula, because we wanted to use God's love like a spatula to peel parents off the ceiling when they'd landed there as the result of a broken dream—a child's death or a child who had come home and said, "Mom, Dad, I'm gay."

While I was out there spreading my joy, as I like to say, Ted and Joanne were enduring their own bone-crushing sorrows. Even though Ted was a dynamic, charismatic Christian who continued to lead many, many people to Christ, he was a sinner, just like the rest of us, and he frequently found himself enmeshed in conflicts. Ted's struggles had begun with early childhood abuse resulting in a lifelong battle with his own sexual identity. Because of this, Joanne and Ted had faced some times of great pain. But this torment was intermingled with many years of joy and the normalcy of a loving, tightly knit family. Ted and Joanne always were aware of the graciousness of a loving God who uses broken earthly vessels to touch other lives for Himself. And that same grace, along with their commitment to each other and their children, helped them maintain a wholesome and nurturing home environment. Their family moved several times, eventually going back to the "lower forty-eight." Their children grew up and married, and Ted and Joanne found themselves living in the Seattle area after their children had settled two thousand miles away. Three or four years ago, the strain of the mounting tension finally caused Joanne and Ted to separate, but they remained close, went through further counseling, and held on to the goal of reconciliation.

A Time of Heartache . . . and Healing

In February 1999 Ted was working for a furniture retailer that transferred him to the state where their children and grandchildren live. In April, Joanne followed, continuing the steps they were taking toward restoring their marriage. Ted was living in a tiny apartment in a small town. Joanne temporarily moved in with their son, Dan, and his wife, Missy, about 150 miles north of Ted. Pam and her family live in between the two towns. Joanne and Ted were hoping to ease back into living together as soon as a new home could be found.

Ted's birthday was Saturday, June 5, and he planned to make the three-hour drive the following Tuesday for a special birthday dinner at Dan and Missy's home. Then they would share the next day together. But Tuesday night came and went, and Ted didn't arrive.

"We had talked to him on Saturday," Joanne recalled. "When he didn't arrive Tuesday afternoon, we thought, well, something's come up. Even on Tuesday evening after he hadn't arrived for the dinner, we thought he would still be coming. But he could not be reached. We tried and tried to call him."

On Wednesday morning, their concern intensified, and Missy called Pam's husband, Eric, asking him to drive to Ted's apartment, which was just an hour's drive away from Eric and Pam's home. Joanne worried that the pressures of all the recent changes might be overwhelming for him. Was he ill? she wondered.

"The apartment was locked when Eric got there, and he could hear the dog whimpering inside," Joanne said. Eric called Joanne. "I'm here at the door, and it's locked," he said. "But I hear the dog. I'm going to get the manager."

The truth was that when he called her he already knew what had happened on the other side of the door, but he just couldn't bring himself to say it on the phone. Joanne called her son, Dan, at work to relay Eric's cryptic message, and Dan sensed that Eric was covering up the truth. He called Eric's cell phone. "What's happened down there?" he asked. And Eric told him.

Dan came home, ashen faced and trembling. Joanne was puttering around the kitchen when Dan walked in and the phone rang simultaneously. "Don't answer that!" he barked.

Then Dan's voice softened, and he said simply, in a state of shock and bewilderment, "Dad's been murdered."

"I slipped in a heap to the floor," Joanne said, "and we cried. It was a time of weeping and agony. Ted was big, strong, capable, smart—and fearless. We just hadn't faced the possibility that something serious could happen to him. He wasn't a door locker. He would just forget about locking the door . . ."

Ted's assailant had been brutal—and deliberate. He had rifled through drawers, sat in a chair, and, as Ted lay dead or dying in the next room, he had helped himself to dinner at the table—had even taken a shower. A friend identified the body so that Joanne and her family were spared the grisly scene.

The accused murderer was apprehended nine days later, tracked down after trading Ted's car for drug money and using Ted's Visa card, checks, and cash.

Then there came the moment when the family gathered for the pretrial hearings and saw, for the first time, the man accused of killing their husband and father. "It was the single most excruciating part of the whole ordeal. My son and daughter were both shaking when he was brought in. He was in shackles. It was an agony to go through."

As the judicial process continued, so did Joanne's heartache—and healing.

Running to God's Word

"I have sought counseling and help here and there," she said. "But that is not what's helped the most. Instead it's just running—*running*—to God in His Word and basking in His presence. I have a little plaque that Ted had on his desk. It says, 'Joy is not in the absence of suffering but in the presence of God.'"

Joanne also says it helps to "journal my heart—record what I am thinking, what I'm going through, and what Scriptures God has given me for *that* day—one day at a time. God gives me the strength and the words from the Scriptures that I hang on to for that day and that occasion. There is no place else for me, in the final analysis, except running to His Word."

She doesn't always start her day by reading the Bible, as many Christians do. "I guess I have to say, contrary to the best teaching, my times in the Word are spontaneous. If I wake up in the morning and feel like turning on a Christian television program or watching the news, I'll do that. If I feel like going out and trimming flowers, I do that. Then I come back in and after a while I pick up the Bible and my notebook and begin to read and rejoice in God's presence or whatever He has to tell me at that moment. I literally am shocked sometimes at how immediately He speaks to me the appropriate words for that particular moment and that day.

"I have received so much understanding and encouragement from the heart cries of David and others in the psalms. I go through certain books of the Bible for a while—Romans, First Peter, Galatians—sometimes pursuing answers on a particular topic or Scripture segment. Then I go through a period when I simply open the Bible and read. I have so many things underlined and noted. It's not a hodgepodge, though. God speaks to me when I open that Book. It's *alive* with His presence, and that's where I choose to live. I've learned how to be there by being forced there, through some of our struggles over the years. I read my journal, reread it, refer back. God still speaks to me through the things He said to me during the week after Ted's death. Sometimes I begin to grieve and sense feelings of failure, but then I remember that God said this or that to me, and it's right here on page so-and-so, because that's where I wrote it down."

The most comforting thing Joanne senses God saying to her is this: "Joanne, Ted's with Me. Forget those hard and painful things and move on!"

Hearing that message, Joanne knows she's come another step in the joy and awareness of God's presence. "Even now, even after all that's happened. Oh, my gracious, yes! It's my life and breath."

And then she shares that life and breath with another hurting woman. Someone tells her of a wife who's enduring a similarly painful trek through the valley of the shadow. And Joanne may write a note or pick up the phone to call and encourage her.

When I asked Joanne if I could share her story here, she wrote that she wanted to share but she was filled with trepidation. "I hurt so, Barbara. My kids hurt. I've lived a lifetime of God's intervention and God's blessing in my life. I know that only He can turn things around, bring beauty for ashes, the oil of gladness for mourning. . . . If God can use my story to make a difference for dear ones who hurt . . . then I want to do it!"

A Comforting Sparkle

This book is about jewels—living, breathing gems who have endured tremendous pressure and overwhelming change to become precious Christians who use their sparkle to bring comfort to others. When I told my friends that I wanted to write this book, they immediately flooded me with all sorts of gemstone charts and books, stories about birthstones—you name it. I was fascinated when I saw that the idea of birthstones—one for every month of the year—may have evolved from the description of the elaborate breastplate described in Exodus 28 and 39, a magnificent piece bearing twelve stones—one for each of the twelve tribes of Israel. One of those stones was a garnet.

Garnet, the Gem of Constant Love

Whenever I see listings of the twelve birthstones, there is garnet, the birthstone for January, right at the beginning. And even though that's not Joanne's birthstone, it is the perfect gem to symbolize her life, because one of its meanings, according to tradition, is constant, long-lasting love. That's the love Joanne has for living in God's presence, and it's the love she shared with Ted despite some anguishing times that made for painful difficulties.

One of the appealing facts I found is that sheets of garnet have been used in stained-glass windows because they diffuse the light with such breathtaking beauty. And legend has it that Noah suspended a garnet in the ark to disperse light. Now, isn't that the perfect description of Joanne, as well? No one I know has dispersed the light of God's Word as enthusiastically as she and Ted have done in their kind, gentle way with their warm, welcoming hospitality. We usually think of garnets as deep reds, but the fact is, the garnet is a "family" of gems, according to one expert, occurring not only as hues of red but also as orange, yellow, pink, green, and brown. And that's like the diverse family of believers Ted and Joanne have nurtured.

When Ted died, Joanne heard from dozens of people whose lives the two of them had touched—strangers and others who had sat at the McReynoldses' dinner table and enjoyed the meal Joanne had so carefully planned or who had relaxed in their living room for discussions about applying God's Word to their lives so that they felt not only nourished but loved.

When Joanne and I were preparing this manuscript, I sent her the first draft of what I had written about her, and, true to her nature, she reminded me that we should add a couple of sentences to explain what it means to be a Christian and how to become one. "These few words could make the difference in someone's life," she said, "and they also explain who I am and have been. Since becoming a Christian at age fifteen, one of my greatest joys is to watch the light go on in those who 'see' for the first time that Jesus died for them and has forgiven their sins (all of them!), and that heaven is their assured destiny. They have just invited Jesus to come into their hearts. Sharing this is my continued desire and future, even more clearly defined now that my husband is *there!*"

This is the message the McReynoldses shared with so many. "Sometimes I think about all the people who've sat at our table and gone on to touch other lives," she said. "For example, one of them was Steve Valentine, who's now a pastor in the West. He told me, 'Every time I give my testimony I talk about you and Ted, and being in your home.' Then he said to me, 'Joanne, we had a plumber come to our house to do some work. We were sharing about when we had met Christ. Lo and behold, this man, this unknown plumber, had also been led to Christ by Ted McReynolds in California.'"

Another friend, Denny Harris, now a minister, wrote, "If it had not been for Ted, I would not know the Lord. I would be lost." They met at the University of California at Berkeley, where Ted and Joanne worked in ministry. "There were times when I truly believed Ted was the only person on campus who really cared about me," Denny said. "Yet when he tried to share Christ with me, I pushed him away. He never stopped trying in spite of the times I canceled appointments, stood him up, . . . pushed him away from the real issues. . . . It was February 27, 1967, in the living room of your apartment that Ted helped me take those first baby steps into the kingdom." Later he added, "Ted made all the difference for me, and every time I tell the story of coming to faith, to the degree that any human is on center stage, that . . . role is reserved for Ted."

At one point, while pastoring a church part-time, Ted also was a high school teacher. One of his former students, who had also lived in Ted and Joanne's home, spoke at Ted's memorial service. She said Ted and Joanne McReynolds were the kind of Christians who were willing to invest themselves in the lives of those who needed help. "They weren't afraid of getting their hands dirty," she said, adding that Ted had led half of the twenty-three students in his class that year to the Lord. Many of them, she said, are now in active Christian service.

"I Know You'd Take This All Back If You Could"

Joanne's story is one of joy and victory, love and heartache. At the last courtroom appearance when the killer was sentenced, Joanne and her family were invited to address the man who had so viciously murdered their loved one.

When the killer, in leg irons and handcuffs, turned and faced them, Pam told him, "I miss my daddy! We had a wonderful, special relationship. I cannot stop thinking about the suffering he went through in his death—the suffering caused by you."

Pam's husband, Eric, said Ted was "my best friend before he was a father-in-law to me." He urged the killer to go to his own parents and tell them he loved them. And he said, "I know you'd take this all back if you could, but it's too late for that."

Ted and Joanne's son, Dan, told the man he wished he had been at Ted's apartment when the attack occurred. "You'd have had to kill me first to get to my dad. . . . You killed the only man I've ever known who would have given his life for me."

The anguished words that tumbled out of their hearts that day expressed abject grief. But there was something else:

When Joanne stood to speak, she noted that Ted had died on his birthday. "I don't think you have any grasp of the agony you've put us through—this family that includes not only our children and their families but Ted's ninety-three-year-old mother, his two brothers, and their families," she said. "I have struggled with this, because God has said I must forgive you. And in my heart I did forgive you, but I still could not say the words until about three months ago. I don't hold any unforgiveness anymore. My prayer for you is that you will find that same forgiveness in Jesus Christ that I have found for my own sins."

By the time everyone left the courtroom area that last morning, Joanne and members of her family had reached out to the convicted man's family with words of comfort and encouragement, knowing that they, too, were in pain. Outside the elevator, Joanne grasped the distraught mother's hand and said, "You'll be in my prayers." The scene so touched a reporter covering the trial that he sent the family a note later, saying, "It was very moving for me as a reporter who has covered murder trials for 20 years to see a family reach out to the family of the man who killed your father the way the McReynolds family has. I have NEVER seen that. I know I never will again."

As pain-filled and intense as this saga has been, there are parts of Joanne's story that, even now, she cannot share. But she has graciously allowed me to tell this much of it, hoping to inspire you and make you aware of the lives you touch every day. Think of Joanne when you share a kind word or a nourishing meal with others, gently giving them the simple yet powerful truth of God's love gift—Jesus. Think of Ted, who, despite his own personal torments, focused on leading lost souls to Christ.

Ted and Joanne touched hundreds of lives—*changed* hundreds of lives. How grateful I am that one of them was my son—a tired, dusty kid from California who stopped for gasoline at the end of the Alaska Highway.

Laughing Through the Tears

Now, let's put a sparkly crystal in those teary eyes, and share a smile or two:

Friends are quiet angels who lift us to our feet when our wings have trouble remembering how to fly.

A sorrow shared is half a trouble,
but joy that's shared is joy made double.[1]

When it comes time to die . . . make sure all you gotta do is die! (Another way of saying, "When God gets ready for you, you'd better be ready for God!")

"I can't really talk right now . . . You-know-who is listening in."

No one is useless in this world
who lightens the burdens of another.

—CHARLES DICKENS

A Christian is one who doesn't have to consult his bank statement to see how wealthy he really is.

A man whispered, "God, speak to me," and a meadowlark
sang. But the man did not hear.

The man yelled, "God, speak to me!" And the thunder rolled
across the sky. But the man did not listen.

The man looked around and said, "God let me see You."
And a star shone brightly. But the man did not notice.

And the man shouted, "God, show me a miracle!" And a life was born. But the man did not know.

So the man cried out in despair, "Touch me, God, and let me know You are here!" Whereupon God reached down and touched the man. But the man brushed the butterfly away and walked on.[2]

You can tell a lot about a person by the way he or she handles:
1. A rainy day
2. Tangled Christmas-tree lights
3. Lost luggage

Niccolo Paganini (1782–1840), one of the greatest violinists of all time, was about to perform before a sold-out opera house. He walked out on the stage to a huge ovation and felt that something was terribly wrong.

Suddenly he realized that he had someone else's violin in his hands. Horrified, but knowing that he had no other choice, he began.

That day he gave the performance of his life.

Afterward, Paganini reflected to a fellow musician, "Today, I learned the most important lesson of my career. Before today, I thought the music was in the violin; today I learned that the music is in *me*."[3]

It's hard to be a fiddle
when you're shaped like a cello.

They that turn many to righteousness will shine as the stars forever and ever. (see Daniel 12:3)

A Broken Heart
Held Together with Laughter

Lynda's gem: *Let God use you to help others. It's the best way to find healing yourself.*

My airhead friend Lynda Wigren often comes with me to Women of Faith conferences to help at my book table. And every trip with her is an adventure, because when Lynda's along, you never know what's going to happen.

You may think it's not nice to call Lynda an "airhead." But that's because you don't know her! She's 100 percent sanguine—full of joy, quick to laugh, and absolutely unconcerned with details. For example, she called me recently to ask if I remembered the name of the doctor she'd been referred to for some tests and if, by chance, I also remembered when the appointment was. I had given her a book to write down her appointments and schedule, but she'd lost it.

She's the only person I know who hasn't bothered to memorize her social security number. She keeps it locked away in a storage chest in the garage!

Last year one conference was held at an arena fourteen miles across the city from the hotel where we were staying. Our local hostess picked us up at the hotel about 4:30 P.M. and fought her way through rush-hour traffic to get us to the arena just as the doors were opening at 5:00. As we hurried to the book table, Lynda gasped. "Oh, Barb!" she said. "I left the money bags back at the hotel!"

The money bags held five- and ten-dollar bills we use for change, and since we don't take plastic at the book table, we knew we were doomed if we didn't have change. It would be too much to hope that everyone would have the exact amount to pay for the books.

Rattled and rushed, Lynda borrowed a friend's car to zoom back to the hotel. The one she ended up with was a stick shift, which Lynda hadn't driven in several years, but of course that was a mere detail, so off she went, unconcerned. All I can say is, I'm glad I wasn't a passenger in that car as she lurched and jumped her way through that rush-hour traffic! When she finally got back to the hotel it suddenly dawned on her that she hadn't left the money bags in her room after all. She had stuck them under the seat in the hostess's car—which was, of course, parked back at the arena!

Love-Filled Misadventures

Wherever Lynda goes, there's laughter—and love. She is bubbling over with passionate love for God and all His children. Last year she went with me to a conference in New Jersey and took a bus tour of New York City the day before the conference. By the time she got back to the hotel that evening, she knew the names and stories of everyone on the bus and had led the driver to the Lord! Of course, she had also gotten lost during the lunchtime break, and she got on the wrong bus after a couple of the sightseeing stops. But none of that caused her any concern at all.

She sometimes accompanies me to the big, Christian booksellers convention. One year I was there, doing a television interview at one of the broadcaster's booths, when Lynda, who had been browsing through the nearby booths, suddenly came running up, shouting to me, "Barb! Barb! You've just gotta see this! It's the most—"

It was then, I suppose, that she felt the heat of the broadcaster's bright stage lights and noticed that I was flashing daggers at her with my eyes. She jerked to a stop right when she reached the spot between the camera and my interviewer and me, her face in a frozen expression of astonishment. "Oh!" she squealed again, turning to look, aghast, right into the camera's lens. Then she backed off the set, found a chair somewhere, and sat with her face hidden in her hands. By then, of course, I was on the verge of hysterical laughter, and so was the interviewer!

Another time Lynda and I were traveling together, waiting in the gate area of the tiny little Ontario, California, airport. We were talking away when it occurred to us that the other chairs around us were now empty and the whole place had grown quiet. "Lynda! What time is it?" I shrieked. (I have to admit, I have quite a few sanguine tendencies myself.)

"Oh, my goodness! They've already boarded!" she yelled.

Out on the tarmac, we could see the ground crew closing the door to a plane—*our* plane—and pulling the stairs away. We gathered up our stuff and went running across the concrete. And believe me, seeing Lynda and me run is *not* something you soon forget!

The crewmen pushed the stairs back up to the plane, opened the door, and, I'm sure, stifled a giggle as we bumbled up the to the plane. We had just gotten seated and heaved one good, long sigh of relief when Lynda suddenly shouted, "Oh, no! I left my purse at the gate!"

Once again the plane's door was reopened, the stairs were pushed back in place, and Lynda hurriedly trotted into the airport to retrieve her purse.

And speaking of Lynda's purse—you should see it! It's always crammed *full* of a million little pieces of paper, each one with the name of someone Lynda wants to send something to—or someone she's promised *I'll* send something to.

Wherever Lynda goes, she talks to everyone. Then she writes down the name of everyone she meets and shoves it into her purse, meaning to send a card or one of my books or something. Some of the little scraps have important phone numbers or rescheduled appointments (because, of course, she forgot the original appointment) or crucial bits of information like flight numbers and hotel addresses. Amazingly, Lynda *does* send dozens of cards to people all over the country—funny cards, touching cards, "I'm thinking of you" cards. But some of those little scraps of paper will never again see the light of day.

One of the memories Lynda and I laugh about most is the time she and I and another friend, Rose, were sharing a limo to the airport, and Lynda had to get out first to catch her flight. Well, if you've ever ridden in a limo, you know that they may *look* sleek and glamorous, but they are nearly impossible to get into and out of unless you're the lucky person seated right by the door. And maybe you've seen television programs that show the movie stars arriving for the Academy Awards, and noticed how gracefully those rail-thin women step out of the car and onto that red carpet. They carefully put their one foot out first (think of that children's song, "Put your little foot, put your little foot . . ."). Well, Lynda had apparently never seen how the starlets did it, because when she tried to get out, it was a disaster!

She weighed a lot more then than she does now, and she attempted to *back* out of the limo, trying to get the biggest part of her out first (rather than her "little foot"). What a sight to behold! A couple of guys standing on the sidewalk nearly collapsed in laughter. Rose pulled, and I pushed, and some passersby asked if they could help. It was obvious we were in trouble! And through it all, Lynda was laughing so hard she nearly wet her pants!

Lynda's Contagious Laughter

To meet Lynda, hear her infectious laughter, and share in her zany misadventures, you would be instantly aware of her giving spirit (and her airheadedness, I might add). People are amazingly drawn to her heart of gold. But seeing the way she sparkles, you might never suspect the trials and the terrible hurts she has known.

As a young woman she went to college, joined a sorority, and, not surprisingly, was immediately put in charge of arranging parties. She met Don, a handsome young marine, and began drinking and using drugs at the many parties they attended. Always fighting a battle with her weight, Lynda began taking Benzedrine—speed. The drug not only helped her lose weight, it made her even more hyper than before. She was caught in a destructive spiral.

Lynda's father owned a bookstore, and when he asked her to leave college to help him in the store, she agreed.

Lynda had gone to church as a child until her mother got mad at the pastor one day, threw her tithing envelopes against the wall—and that was the end of that. So when someone came into the bookstore one day and gave her a book—the Gospel of John—she dropped it into her purse and forgot it (like she forgets everything else). One night at a party, Lynda wasn't drinking as much as usual. She found herself in the bathroom, digging through her purse—and found the Gospel of John. Despite repeated pounding on the door, she stayed in the bathroom until she'd read the whole booklet. The back cover told her what she had to do to be saved. "As dawn came, I probably repented for two hours," she said.

Then she asked Jesus to come into her heart. Lynda had worn a bright red taffeta dress to the party, and as the veil lifted from her spiritual eyes, she thought to herself, *Wouldn't it be neat if God gave me some kind of sign that He'd heard me?* As the sun rose, she walked outside—and came upon one little flower. It was red, the color of her dress. She felt sure God had grown that flower that very morning just for her.

Babysteps toward Heaven

She and Don were married a few months later. And gradually, with God's help and a great deal of determination, Lynda gave up the drugs and alcohol. Their first daughter, Denise, was born nine months after their wedding. Cheryl came two and a half years later. When Cheryl was born, "everything was wrong," Lynda said. Her spine had not closed off. Her hips were out of joint. One foot was turned out and twisted into a U shape. She had mental retardation and a condition known as a "floating" eye.

For three years, Lynda and Don struggled to cope with Denise, their active toddler, and Cheryl, their infant afflicted with multiple problems. During those years, they both knew heartache and triumph.

"Right away the doctors put Cheryl's leg in a tiny little cast and said they would have to keep putting her in casts as she grew so that her foot would straighten out," Lynda said. "All this time I prayed and trusted the Lord. I read my Bible and just let Him fill me with faith. The second time I took Cheryl in to have a new cast put on, they cut the old cast off—and her foot was okay! She didn't need another cast. Then they said she needed a special brace for her hips; both hips could easily be pulled out of joint. They put a special brace on her little legs, but she cried all night, and I just couldn't stand to see her suffer. So I took off the brace, and I never put it back on. Finally I took her to the doctor, and he could not pull either hip out of joint. He thought the brace had corrected the problem, but I knew she hadn't been wearing the brace after the first night."

Don and Lynda had no health insurance, and he was working two jobs seven days a week to try to make ends meet. While Lynda stayed home with the girls, Don worked at his father-in-law's bookstore. Each day when the bookstore closed, he walked across the street to a gas station to begin his second job. And through it all, he continued to drink heavily.

The family was helped tremendously by a Shriners hospital and by the City of Hope Medical Center, where compassionate doctors let them make payments on their soaring bills. And Lynda worked with her little daughter constantly. Her next goal was to teach Cheryl to talk. Lynda especially wanted to hear her little girl say the name of Jesus.

"Cheryl had so many problems, but the Lord took us step

by step as He healed her so that we would pray and see His glory," Lynda said. The doctors said she would not walk until she was five—if at all. But by age two, Cheryl was toddling all over the house.

Then came the biggest setback. When she was three and a half, Cheryl was diagnosed with leukemia. The doctors gave her two weeks, but she lived a month. Throughout those agonizing weeks, the little girl suffered great pain, and then she slipped into a coma. Lynda was with Cheryl constantly; she was there on that last evening when the little girl suddenly sat up and cried out, "DeeDee! DeeDee!"

Lynda thought Cheryl was calling for her sister, Denise. She ran out of the room to call Don, and when she came back, Cheryl had died.

Those were dark days for Lynda and Don, but Lynda clung to her faith. She had so wished to hear her sweet little daughter speak the name of Jesus, but it hadn't happened. Then one day Lynda's sister, Terri, came over and brought her own little girl, who was about Cheryl's age. As they were chitchatting, Terri was trying to get her daughter to show Lynda how many words she could say. "Tell Aunt Lynda how you say Jesus," Lynda's sister instructed.

"DeeDee!" the little girl answered joyfully.

"That's how she says Jesus?" Lynda asked, stunned.

Her sister nodded, and Lynda realized that in her last moments with little Cheryl, when the little girl had suddenly sat up and cried out, "DeeDee! DeeDee!" she hadn't been calling for her big sister after all. She'd been saying the name "Jesus."

My Devoted Encourager

Lynda's life has been punctuated by tragedy, soothed by God's peace, and flooded with joy, especially when their son, Steve, was born in 1967.

A few years later, Lynda went back to work part-time at a Berean bookstore, where I became one of her regular customers—and was blessed by the friendship that quickly developed between us. You see, Lynda doesn't just stand behind a counter and peddle books. She ministers to everyone who steps through the door. It might just be a sweet hello and a bright smile—or it might be a heartfelt time of sharing, when some heartbroken person pours out a story of pain. Whatever the situation, Lynda always has just the right word of Christian encouragement and God's hope.

She was there the day I came into the store in 1979 as I was completing my very first book, *Where Does a Mother Go to Resign?* The publisher had balked at the title I wanted and wanted to rename it *Where Do You Go to Mend a Broken Heart?*, which was nothing like what I wanted. In the bookstore that day, I explained my dilemma to Lynda, and she came to my defense and insisted I hang in there with the title I had chosen. Knowing her years of experience in bookstores and marketing, I was reassured that my chosen title was best and that I should be firm with the publisher. Since then, I have heeded her advice about my books, because I know she's an expert. She's also well known throughout the bookstore industry in Southern California. She knows everyone, and everyone seems to know her.

After my first book was published, Lynda sent a tape of one of my speaking engagements and some of my material to a bigger publishing house that she said published the kind of books I could write. She urged that company to publish my next book, but her proposal was rejected. The acquisitions manager said in his reply that my material was not suitable for that publisher's targeted readers. So my next book, *Fresh Elastic for Stretched-Out Moms,* was published by someone else. But it turned out that Lynda was right. Soon after that second book was published, W Publishing Group, the company Lynda had sent my stuff to, approached me with a contract for *Stick a Geranium in Your Hat and Be Happy.* W has published nearly all my books since then. And that first letter from W, rejecting Lynda's proposal, is framed and hanging on the wall in my Joy Room.

Lynda has been my most devoted encourager and friend. Knowing how I love to laugh, she calls frequently to share a funny joke or story she's heard—or to confess some silly thing she's done. When she travels with me to speaking engagements, she exudes a love for others that is remarkable to behold. Having her at my book table is a blessing to all the brokenhearted women who make their way through the crowds in search of an understanding heart, the perfect word of Scripture to bring joy to those lost in the darkness—and a hug.

Harvesting the Seeds of Joy

One day Lynda was driving with me to a speaking engagement in California when I had grown weary of all the traveling and the pressure. We were riding in the car, and I suddenly spouted off. "Oh, Lynda, I'm so *sick* of spreading my joy—sick, sick, sick!"

We both erupted in laughter—I'm sure Lynda laughed first. Then I said, more seriously, "Lynda, I think I'm getting burned out. It's getting harder and harder to spread my joy."

And just then we looked up and saw a huge, fifty-foot billboard that said in bold letters: "SPREAD YOUR JOY!" It was as if God were speaking directly to me in a big, loud voice. We laughed all the way to the church.

The church had said the price of admission to this event was an unsaved friend. You couldn't get in unless you brought someone who didn't know the Lord. I was down at the front of the church, getting ready to speak, and Lynda was out in the foyer, setting up the book table, when she looked up to see a woman leading another woman by the hand. "She just looked like a zombie," Lynda said. "She didn't really even look like she was alive. The other woman led her into the auditorium, and she was just following like a robot."

In a few moments the "leading" lady, apparently having seated her zombie friend, reappeared at the book table. "Oh, I just hope that whatever Barb has to say today helps my friend," the woman said. "Her little eight-year-old boy recently hung himself."

Lynda's face must have shown her anguished shock, because the woman hurried to add, "I'm sure he didn't mean to.

You know how kids are. They just do stuff and they don't know the consequences. I just hope what Barb says helps her."

Lynda squeezed the woman's hand in both of hers. "Oh, I'll be praying with you that it does."

Later, at the end of the meeting, Lynda saw the boy's mother coming out of the auditorium. "She was walking like she was alive again," Lynda said. "Her head was up, and she almost seemed to have a little spark in her eye. I just couldn't help myself. I thought, *I've just gotta talk to her.* So I went over to her and said, 'I know you've gone through such an awful time lately. I'm so sorry. I hope what Barb said helped you.'"

The woman put her hands together as if she were in prayer and said, "Oh! She's given me such hope. She's given me such *hope!*"

Afterward, Lynda made a tape of this story—she calls it her favorite Barb story. And on the tape she says, "Oh, Barb! That's what your ministry is about—giving hope to people. I mean, you may joke that you have no faith, Barb, but you sure have a lot of hope: Hope that the Lord is coming, hope that we're going to heaven. And you instill that hope into people so they can keep going, no matter what. So bless you, my dear friend, for your ministry. You've gotten me through so many painful experiences; I'd never have survived them without hope. And that hope's still alive and bright because of you. Thank you!"

One Last Good-bye

Lynda had already survived some horrendous challenges when I met her—heavy drug and alcohol use, the death of a beloved child, the destruction of the family business—once by fire and next by an earthquake—and life with a loving but heavy-drinking husband. So I had little to do with her survival; that was the Lord's work, not mine. But I was there during some other times in recent years that were just as tragic. The worst came two years ago when Lynda got the call that her fun-loving, fifteen-year-old grandson, Shaun, had been terribly injured in a fiery explosion.

Shaun and Lynda had been kindred spirits who loved a

hearty belly laugh more than anything else. When he was fourteen, the two of them had stood in a line of parents and toddlers for nearly an hour to have their picture taken together with Santa Claus. They loved to go to comedy movies together—preferably the late shows so they could laugh and carry on and no one would complain about all the noise they made. He cheerfully played cards with Lynda's aging mother.

But Shaun's most favorite thing was fireworks. He loved all the noise and color of the Fourth of July, and Lynda and Shaun's parents always made sure they had a big "show" for the holiday. But Shaun's fascination with explosives carried him into danger when a sixteen-year-old friend discovered Internet instructions for making a pipe bomb.

"They had no concept of what they were doing," Lynda said. "To them it was just a big fireworks thing. The whole group of neighborhood kids knew about it—in fact, the two boys worked on it out in front of the house, out in the street. They apparently had no idea that it was a bad thing. They just knew to run real fast when it went off."

But Shaun didn't run fast enough.

He died in the ambulance, but the paramedics revived him. He survived another day and was taken into surgery. But the doctors soon appeared and told the grieving family that Shaun was too far gone.

"Not too long before that, a neighbor had died because no heart had been available for transplant," Lynda said. "Shaun had been beside himself. He and his sister, April, had said several times since then that they wanted to be organ donors. So we knew at that point what Shaun would want us to do."

The medical staff gratefully shifted gears and started the transplant process, notifying recipients and scheduling facilities. At this point Shaun was alive only because of the machines attached to his body, but even then his body was shutting down. They waited as long as they could, but soon the hospital chaplain came to the grieving family and friends—nearly twenty people who huddled, heartbroken, in the hallway outside the Intensive Care wing.

"It's time," he told them gently. "We have to move quickly. They're going to shut off the life-support machines and take Shaun back into the OR. I'm afraid they won't be able to stop, but we'll wheel him by here . . . for one last good-bye."

Standing together in the middle of the hallway, Lynda held her daughter, Denise, Shaun's mother, as the medical team hurriedly pushed the gurney just beyond the reach of the distraught mother's outstretched hand.

"She was crying so hard, 'Mom! Mom! What am I going to do?'" Lynda said. "And I was holding her in my arms and crying just as hard. All I could say was, 'I don't know, Honey. I don't know.' And just then I felt God the Father wrap His arms around us and whisper in my ear: *I understand. I watched My Son die, too.*"

The experience gave Lynda a whole new revelation of God's love. She realized that God had watched as His own Son was being led away to Calvary. As Lynda glimpsed her beloved grandson for the last time, the impact of God's sacrifice was made real.

Laughing at Heaven's Gate

Healing came slowly. But even as they mourned Shaun's death, the heartbroken family struggled to cope with another dilemma—Lynda's mother's last illness. On the same day the pipe bomb had exploded, her mother had been hospitalized due to a fall. Suffering from terrible pain, her mother was slipping in and out of consciousness, and the family had not told her that her great-grandson had been killed.

Now, you might think that this set of tragedies might completely erode a normal person's sense of humor. But, of course, Lynda is anything but normal. On her mother's last day, Lynda held her soft, cool hand and said, "I love you, Mommy." And her mother managed to whisper, "I love you, too."

And then Lynda, realizing her mother was slipping away from her, just had to spill the beans. She leaned close to her face and told her, "Mommy, when you get to heaven, there's going to be a big surprise for you!"

Later, Lynda explained, "I just couldn't let her get to heaven and say, 'Shaun! What are *you* doing here?'!"

Lynda and Terri sat by their mother's side as she slowly slipped over the edge into unconsciousness. At that time, Terri lived across the country from Lynda and their parents, and since she didn't get to spend as much time with their mother as Lynda did, she wasn't in on all the little customs and jokes they had shared. She wasn't aware that a favorite gospel song about heaven that Lynda and her mother loved to sing had the phrase "Meet me at the eastern gate." As their mother slipped into the final coma, Lynda again leaned down to their mother's peaceful face and said, "Remember, Mommy, we'll meet at the eastern gate."

"WHAT?!" her sister exclaimed. "No one told me about meeting at the eastern gate. Who decided it would be the *eastern* gate? If nobody'd told me, I'd probably be waiting at the *western* gate, asking Jesus, 'Where *is* everybody?'!"

Their mother, perhaps even as she heard the heavenly chorus singing that beloved hymn, lay on her deathbed and laughed with her daughters.

These days, except for Lynda's persistent airheaded forgetfulness, Don and Lynda's life is on a more even keel. Don quit drinking nearly eight years ago, and today they both work for a Christian bookstore in Whittier, California. It's a setting that gives Lynda a chance to share the gospel—and the sheer joy of believing—with hundreds of people whose paths cross hers. And one of the things she tells those who come to her with broken hearts is the philosophy that has helped her become one of God's precious jewels. "Let God use you to help others," she says. "It's the best way to find healing yourself."

God's Thumbprint on Lynda's Heart

Three weeks after her grandson, Shaun, died, Lynda was working in the back of the store when the manager asked her to step out front to talk to a distraught woman whose sixteen-year-old daughter had recently died. Lynda listened to the woman pour out her story, and she shared loving and encouraging words with her. Then Lynda told her about books written by a woman named Barbara Johnson, who had survived the deaths of two sons and the alienation of a third son after they'd argued over his homosexuality. The woman's tears flowed anew. "My daughter . . . ," she said, in between the sobs, "committed suicide because she thought she was a lesbian."

Several months later, Lynda was working at my book table at a Women of Faith conference when the same woman appeared in front of her. After she'd reintroduced herself, she told Lynda, "I'm here because of you and because of Barbara Johnson."

"Oh! I hope you've been helped by what you've heard," Lynda said, pulling her into a hug.

"Oh, yes," the woman smiled, her eyes sparkling. "Oh, yes."

Lynda's truly a gem. Her life reminds me of a beautiful amethyst, the birthstone appointed for February. Tradition says the sparkling amethyst was worn to "guard against drunkenness," and Lynda had to battle that terrible problem during her wild years. Thank goodness she had a much more powerful Rock to help her conquer that challenge! But the thing about the amethyst that reminds me most about Lynda is what's inside her. In the same way, there are some distinctive markings, or "inclusions," in this gemstone that help jewelers identify it. One of those distinctive inclusions looks like a thumbprint. And that's Lynda. You may not notice it at first when you observe her giggles and scatterbrained forgetfulness. But when you look a little deeper, you see the distinctive mark that emphatically identifies her. It is the thumbprint of the Father upon her heart.

Laughing Through the Tears

No story about Lynda is complete without a big bunch of laughter. She is living fulfillment of Job 8:21: "He will yet fill your mouth with laughter and your lips with shouts of joy." Here's a cartoon that made us both laugh out loud:

CLOSE TO HOME By John McPherson

Nellie tries out her miracle bra.

Always remember this: A positive attitude may not solve all your problems . . . but it will annoy enough people to make it worth the effort!

We've reached the age where just haulin' our fat around counts as a workout.

Best time to be happy: *now.*
Best place to be happy: *here!*

The best things are nearest: Breath in your nostrils, light in your eyes, flowers at your feet, duties at your hand, the path of God just before you.

—ROBERT LOUIS STEVENSON

After attending his first Women of Faith conference, one of my friends, Rafael Chacon, drew this sketch of the craziness that sometimes surrounds my book table—a scene Lynda knows very well!

A greeting-card line you'll never see:
I'm so miserable without you, it's almost like you're here.

You're blessed when you're at the end of your rope. With less of you there is more of God and his rule. (Matthew 5:3 MSG)

Sharing the Wealth of God's Unconditional Love

Maggie's gem: *When you stand before God, He's not going to ask you what your child did. He's going to ask you what you did.*

Sometimes when I'm working at speaking engagements, I make my way from the podium to the book table and find Maggie Stillman already at work there with the other women who travel with me occasionally. I watch for a moment, taking in the scene and marveling at the ministry Maggie has chosen for herself—especially considering what she *could* be doing instead.

Maggie could be relaxing on the ski slopes or some tropical island or hanging out at the country club after a round of golf or a set of tennis. In fact, she does enjoy some of those things infrequently. Maggie and her husband have ample resources to retire and make any of those leisure-time hobbies their full-time routine. Instead, often as not, she spends a lot of her free time and pays all her own expenses to join me at speaking sites around the country.

My book table is always a magnet for women who long to pour out their anguish about a child who is gay or a child who has died. My speaking duties keep me away from the table most of the time, but often I'm blessed to have kindhearted friends who travel with me and who work at my table, offering their own loving sympathy to these hurting women. Some of these friends, like Lynda Wigren and Nancy Bryson (whom you'll meet later), have lost children or grandchildren and use their experiences to reach out to those in similar circumstances. Maggie has a gay daughter. And like the other friends, she may stand there for hours, selling books, of course, but also waiting for God to guide another brokenhearted mom her way.

Always perfectly dressed in her stylish outfits and designer shoes, Maggie patiently listens and works with women of all means and demeanors—wealthy socialites and welfare mothers, full-time homemakers and high-level executives—all relieved to find someone with whom they can share their broken dream or their embarrassing secret. In Maggie they find someone who will listen without judging as they pour out their stories. What relief these women feel when they nervously approach my table, hint at what's on their hearts, and then see that warm spark of recognition and concern in Maggie's eyes. She leads them to a quiet spot—or as quiet as it gets in these crowded arenas—where they can talk, and soon they feel comforted and understood. They're encouraged to meet someone who has such a bright smile and ready laugh and then to realize that her heart has been broken, too.

Making the Choice to Share and Serve

Maggie doesn't just work with me on the road. When she's at home, she spends many hours on the phone, helping the distraught mothers I've referred to her. To understand her gift, I have to remind you again that it's not that Maggie has nothing else to do. She and her husband are very actively engaged in their own separate businesses, and they have several adult children and grandchildren with whom they are very close. But Maggie *chooses* to spend much of her free time reaching out to those in need and comforting them with the same comfort she has received from God's Word, especially 2 Corinthians 1:4. It says God "comforts us in all our troubles, so that we can comfort those in any trouble with the comfort we ourselves have received from God." Sharing this promise, says Maggie, is a healing experience in itself.

On a cataclysmic day several years ago, Maggie learned that her daughter, Katherine, is homosexual. "I can barely remember exactly how I came upon the letter. God is so great to let me forget!" she said with a little laugh. "But I had been visiting Katherine in college in a city where I was also doing some business, and somewhere I picked up the letter—I can't remember who the letter was to or who it was from or even why it caught my eye—but I picked it up and shoved it in my purse. I did some things I shouldn't have done back then, and that was one of them. But I was rushing to go somewhere with my friend, Sandy, who had come with me on this trip.

"As I was driving, I pulled out the letter and asked her to read it to me. And everything after that is a blur . . . I can't even remember what the letter said. But it let me know for sure that Katherine was gay. I guess the miracle that day was that I managed to get the car off the Interstate without having a wreck and killing us both."

Sandy, the friend who was with Maggie that day, let Maggie cry and shriek and moan without interrupting. "She didn't say anything for a long time, except those little sounds friends make: 'Uh-huh,' and 'Ahhh,' and 'I'm so sorry.' She just listened to me go on and on about how this couldn't be true and about how devastating this news was to me. She let me rant and rave that we would simply 'fix' Katherine, make her *not* be homosexual. I was sure we could change her somehow."

Remarkably, Maggie made it through the day, blindly stumbling through business appointments in a daze of hurt and bewilderment. Today, many years later, she doesn't remember the trip home at all, and she can't remember telling her husband the news. One of the next scenes in her memory of that time is sitting outside her home church sobbing and sobbing to her pastor.

The pastor recommended Christian counseling for Katherine, and Maggie and her husband quickly agreed. They flew back to Katherine's college town to confront her. As they neared the campus, Maggie continually recited a verse Sandy had given her, 2 Timothy 1:7 (NKJV): "For God has not given us a spirit of fear, but of power and of love and of a sound mind." The thing she remembers now about that confrontation was "that there were lots of tears. I said things I wish I wouldn't have said, and Katherine basically just sat and cried. She's the kind of person who won't defend herself. She's always been so easygoing and softspoken."

After their tearful meeting, the family began a long, agonizing project to "fix" their daughter. Incredibly, during that period, they flew their daughter home from college nearly every weekend for two years so that she could meet with a counselor. Amazingly, their beautiful, sweet daughter willingly complied with this hectic, pressure-filled schedule. "Katherine would have done anything I asked. She is a very loving, thoughtful daughter—very quiet and classy. She's not outwardly gay the way some homosexuals are. In fact, if you met her, you'd probably never suspect it. And she was so tough, enduring all that we put her through. She knew she was gay, yet she tried whatever we asked of her to try to *not* be gay. Now, years later, her partner has told us how hard that period was on Katherine, but she never makes reference to it."

Overwhelmed with Guilt and Shame

During that time, Maggie, her husband, Katherine, and the counselor flew together to a seminar in St. Louis led by some former homosexuals who had come out of the lifestyle. "They said, 'For gay women, it's the overbearing, controlling mother's influence that has primarily caused the homosexuality.' I remember sobbing to Katherine and telling her I was so sorry and asking her forgiveness if I had done anything to drive her in that direction. She insisted it wasn't me. She said, 'I don't think you had anything to do with it.'"

Despite Katherine's reassurance, Maggie wallowed in the guilt that almost all of us mothers of homosexuals have felt at one time or another. "I was overwhelmed with it," Maggie said. "The guilt feelings just went on and on. All I could think about was what I might have done to make her this way. We were so ashamed, we wouldn't tell anyone. Thank goodness Sandy, my trustworthy Christian friend, was with me when I found out about Katherine, because I had her to talk with, pray with, and cry with. We also had our pastor and the counselor. Those were the only people who knew for at least ten years. Sometimes we felt so hopeless and isolated. I can't express with words the value of a true Christian friend in whom you can confide and one who will continually point you to Christ."

Throughout this concerted effort to make Katherine "normal," Sandy was quietly repeating one fact that Maggie did not like to hear but one that she had told Maggie right from the beginning. "She would say, very gently, 'You know, this is one of the most difficult areas to change. Most homosexuals do not come out of the lifestyle,'" Maggie said. "Mostly, though, she just listened to me and prayed for all of us. And she gave me Barb's book: *Stick a Geranium in Your Hat and Be Happy.*"

In my book, Maggie read my own disastrous story of trying to fix my homosexual son, Larry. My misguided words and biblical threats drove him away from our home, and he was estranged from us for eleven years. He changed his name and said he never wanted to speak to us again, and much of the time we didn't even know if he was dead or alive. Maggie went through equally trying experiences. "There were lots of tears, lots of anger, and lots of times—virtually every time I spoke with Katherine—when I should have had a sock stuffed in my mouth so I wouldn't have said the things I said to her."

The next few years were like an emotional roller coaster for Maggie and her husband. "There were times when she'd come out of counseling and we would think she was 'fixed.' We'd send her back to college full of hope and good feelings—and then things would flare up again, and I'd reach for that dog-eared copy of *Geranium*."

"God Softened My Heart"

Maggie admits now that at first she was "as nasty as I could be" toward Katherine's partners. "One time Katherine brought one of them home, and once I realized the situation, I tried to ignore the girl. I'm not proud of it now, but I was just flat-out obnoxious. When I would call their house, if the partner answered, I wouldn't even speak to her. I was really awful. Then what had happened to Barb happened to me. My daughter didn't change, but I changed. God softened my heart through the conversations, prayers, and compassionate ministry of Barbara Johnson, and I realized I was jeopardizing my relationship with this child I loved so much."

About the time Maggie was making that change, Katherine fell in love with another woman—a zany character named Robin who had a feisty, fun-loving personality. To Maggie's amazement, she found herself liking this new partner.

"She just has a great personality," Maggie said. "She's funny and fun to be with. She was very nice to us. I guess you could say she courted us, getting to know us and reassuring us that she loved Katherine as much as we did. In fact, I found myself talking to her on the phone for an hour or two at a time whenever she called. We would just chat and laugh and have a good time."

Finally, Maggie began to accept where Katherine was in her life and that she couldn't force her to change. "I came to a point where I said to myself, 'If that's the way she's gonna live, then I'm gonna love her and leave it to God to convict her to live a life that is honoring to Him.'" Then came the day when Robin met Maggie and blurted out, "I'm in love with your daughter. I want her to move in with me, and I want us to raise children together." Then she paused and asked, "So, Maggie, how do you feel about that?"

Her heart in her throat, Maggie could only stutter, "I'm so glad I've just had two glasses of wine—and I wish someone would bring me the rest of the bottle!"

Two months later, Robin and Katherine invited Maggie and her husband to meet them for dinner. After Maggie's husband asked the blessing, Robin announced, "We're going to have a commitment ceremony. Will you come?"

"I asked her, 'What will you do? Will you kiss and be all over each other?' And she said, 'Well, what if we do?' I told her, 'I would be uncomfortable.' 'Then we won't do that,' Robin said. It was quiet for a moment, and then my husband looked at me and said, 'Well, I haven't discussed this with you, Maggie, but if they're going to have a commitment ceremony, I'll go.' And I said, 'Then I'll go, too.'"

God's Marvelous Way

Back in their hometown, Maggie and her husband decided to tell another couple—some of her closest Christian friends. When Maggie told them about Katherine, she burst into tears, but the friends quickly reassured her. The wife later informed Maggie that their son, who had gone to school with Katherine, had known for years that she was gay—but had never thought it appropriate to mention it to the parents, because it was Katherine's responsibility to do so. Then the woman, concerned, said, "Maggie, why don't you call Barbara Johnson? She's coming to town with the Women of Faith conference. Maybe you could invite her for lunch and talk to her."

Maggie did call me—but like so many others, she got the *other* Barbara Johnson in La Habra, California, by mistake. "She said, 'This is the twentieth call I've had for her today, but I'll give you her number,'" Maggie recalled with a laugh.

We did meet for lunch when the Women of Faith tour rolled into her town. She poured out her heart, and I reassured her that she was doing the right thing to accept the partner and welcome her into their home, therefore keeping her relationship with Katherine intact. I told her she could extend Christ's love to others without condoning their behavior. Then I urged her to come to the program that night. Now I laugh every time Maggie tells about what happened.

"Generally, I dislike women's meetings. But I had wanted to see Barbara and find out what it was all about, so a couple of weeks before the date, I called at least ten people and asked them to go with me to the conference, but it was a holiday weekend, and everyone had other plans. So I had just bought a single ticket. I thought I would stick my head in and if it was bad, I'd come home. After I met Barb and she was so enthusiastic about my going, I told my husband, 'I can't get out of it. Barbara came and had lunch and gave me advice, and I just feel obligated.' So I went, and it was wonderful. And after the speaking sessions, I went to Barb's table and watched what she did, saw how she listened and consoled the women who came to her and how she offered them hope and humor. She was listening to a woman at the table and she called me over and said to the woman, 'This lady needs to talk to you.' Barb nodded for me to listen to the woman while she stood right next to me with her arm around me, supporting me, nodding and smiling, and I just listened compassionately to the woman's story. I guess Barb was satisfied that everything was okay, because she backed off, and I continued listening and responding—with tears in my eyes most of the time. It was a very rewarding and encouraging experience. And I marvel at the way God was involved. If I had been with one of the ten friends I had called to go with me, I wouldn't have had such an opportunity to be mentored and encouraged by Barb. But I went alone, and I guess He and Barb saw fit to use me."

That was four years ago. Since then, God and I have continued to use Maggie whenever she has joined me at speaking engagements around the country. She has assembled material from my books and other resources, and she gladly shares it with the mothers who stagger up to the book table, looking for a lifeline. She also responds when I forward to her the letters of women who have gay daughters and don't know what to do or where to turn. She's a good listener, a strong encourager, and a selfless worker.

Ironically, her daughter and her partner don't know the work Maggie does. She's very careful to protect their identities, and she is also careful not to "preach" to them every time they're together. Before every visit she whispers a quick scriptural prayer, "May the words of my mouth and the meditation of my heart be acceptable in your sight, O LORD, my Rock and my Redeemer" (Psalm 19:14). And she knows her prayers are being heard. One time, Robin asked Maggie, rather condescendingly, "Maggie, do you still pray every day that I won't be gay?" and Maggie answered, "You know, Robin, actually I pray that you'll come to know Jesus Christ as your Lord and Savior." Maggie said later, "I'm telling you, this extremely verbal woman looked at me and was totally speechless. She didn't have a clue how to answer me back."

Words of Advice to Other Mothers

Here's some of the advice Maggie offers from her own learning experiences:

- "When I talk to parents who have just found out their child is gay, I say, 'Consider your child's needs before your own. Find out what your child is feeling and listen to him or her. Your priority is in retaining the relationship with your child and not in persuading him or her to get out of homosexuality.'"

- "Create a solid foundation for your relationship with your child, then keep that relationship alive and let God deal with the rest. Agree to disagree and then find things to do together and things to talk about that don't focus on homosexuality."

- "Remember, when you stand before God, He's not going to ask you what your child did. He's going to ask you what *you* did. For me, it's been one of those blessed ironies. My own personal relationship with God has grown so much stronger since I found out Katherine is gay. I've had to do some work to figure out what I really

believe and resolve how I am going to act. I'm more
grounded now; my faith has grown deeper. And this
experience has taught me to give up control and turn it
all over to God. As Barb says, I'm constantly praying the
prayer of relinquishment: 'Whatever, Lord!'"

• "The hardest thing for many parents is that they fear
they're compromising their Christian ideals and beliefs
when they accept their gay child's lifestyle and when
they love their child's partner. They're so afraid their
child will say, 'Oh, my mother thinks it's okay that I'm
gay.' I tell them, 'You're *not* compromising your beliefs.
Your child will never think that you believe it's okay. But
he or she will be reassured of your unconditional love.
And you can pray that he or she will understand that
you are modeling the kind of love Christ shows for all of
us. We can *accept* a person without *approving* of his or her
behavior.'"

• "Think about the story of Jesus and Zacchaeus, as told in
Luke 19:1–9. The footnotes in my *Life Application Bible*
say, 'Despite the fact that Zacchaeus was both a cheater
and a turncoat, Jesus loved him; and in response, the
little tax collector was converted. . . . We should not give
in to social pressure to avoid [such] people. Jesus loves
them, and they need to hear His Good News.' How was
Zacchaeus going to come to know Christ if Jesus didn't
have anything to do with him? I try to be with Katherine
and her partner whenever they invite me to come, and
we've enjoyed having them in our home. I don't preach
to them, but they know how I feel and what I believe.
One night Robin and I were having a big discussion.
Robin said, 'You Christians are so arrogant. You think
you're the only way to God.' At first I couldn't answer.
Then I tried to tell her it's something that's in your heart,
a personal decision, and that the Bible says Jesus is the
way, the truth, and the life and no one comes to the
Father except through Him. After more exasperating

conversation, I finally told her, 'I don't know too much about the Buddhists or the Muslims or all those other religions, but if I were you, I'd bank on the One who rose from the dead!'"

- "As Christian parents we have the opportunity to be the salt and light in our children's lives. If we, their Christian parents who love them the most, don't demonstrate Christian love to them and reach out to them, why would they ever go to church, ever go to Christian counseling, ever turn to Christ? They would just have no reason to do so if the people who love them the most don't channel God's love to them. There's a line in Philip Yancey's book *What's So Amazing About Grace?* that says, 'We only love Christ as much as we love that person that we love the least.' He loves them more than we do. He has greater resources than we do. He desires the best for them more than we do. As parents we should work to love them for who they are and forgive them for who they're not."

- "I like to share what Sandy has shared with me many times from Philippians 4:8: Keep your mind on things that are noble and right and pure and lovely. Sandy would say to me, 'Stop thinking about what they're doing; get your mind off of the muck of homosexuality and focus on something greater.' Today I focus on being the light to my daughter, her partner, and her partner's adopted children. I consider myself the grandmother of those little ones, and I'm sad that they aren't being raised in the church. I pray for Robin and her children to come to know Christ, and every chance I get, I try to plant a subtle little seed. For example, one day I was keeping one of the children, and he was watching a cartoon video. I said, 'You know, I have a really cool video. You wanna watch it with me?' It was an animated story of the Nativity, and as we watched it together, I silently prayed, *Please, Lord, let this child be remotely interested in this.* And sure enough, when it was over, he asked, 'Can we watch it again?' And later he asked, 'Where's the rest of it? The part about Jesus growing up?' I promised to bring it the next time I visited him, and I whispered another prayer: 'Thank You, Lord!'"

Maggie's story reminds me of the beautiful opal. Made of silica, the opal might have remained nothing more than an ordinary hodgepodge of elements comprising a hunk of lackluster rock, but something cataclysmically wonderful happened to it deep in the earth's darkness. As a result, its milky-white base is infused with a variety of brilliant colors that jewelers call flashes. This play of color can be muted and subdued, or it can gleam like a magical flame. The Borsheim's guide sheet shares a tale that says the opal "was created when God completed painting the universe, scraping the palette and dumping all the colors into one gem."

Something Painfully Wonderful

That's so similar to the way Maggie's story evolves. She could have lived out her life as an ordinary hodgepodge of feelings and emotions, enduring the hurt of having a homosexual daughter by withdrawing from her daughter and from the world around her. But instead, something painfully wonderful happened on the ragged edges of her broken heart, and the result is a brilliant flame of love that has colored her life and the lives of those around her with enduring grace and joy.

And here's another interesting thing about the opal: It is known to "fill cavities" in other rocks and even to form stalagmites or stalactites in caves. It sometimes replaces the organic material in fossilized wood, shell, and bone so that they retain their original shape but begin to gleam with a beautiful opalescence. In the same way, Maggie seeks to replace the hurt and bitterness in other mothers' hearts with the same feelings of peace and confidence she now enjoys. And she carefully oozes Christian love into the lives of her daughter, her daughter's partner, and the children. As slowly and surely as gentle, persistent droplets of silica create beautiful stalactites in a cave, she gently but persistently drops whispers of God's love into the lives of her loved ones, patiently waiting for the moment when the particles of His promises erupt into a fiery flash that ignites their hearts and wins their souls.

My favorite story about the opal is the one that reminds me of the change God worked in Maggie's own heart since she first learned of her daughter's homosexuality. It is said that the opal is merely a pretty stone when it rests in the display case. But when it is picked up and held, its beautiful colors become strikingly visible in the warmth of the jeweler's hand. Maggie understands that transition, for she, too has been changed by the warm, loving touch of the Master.

Laughing Through the Tears

Today, Maggy's a happy, cheerful, outgoing woman who loves to laugh. Here are some of the funny cartoons and jokes we've shared:

A woman called the utility company and complained that her electricity was out. What should she do? The voice on the other end advised, "Open your freezer and eat the ice cream."[1]

If you pursue happiness, it will elude you. But if you focus on your faith, your family, your friends, the needs of others, your work, and do the very best you can, happiness will find you.

God is too good to be unkind and He is too wise to be mistaken. And when we cannot trace His hand, we must trust His heart.

—CHARLES HADDON SPURGEON

RALPH   By Wayne Stayskal

When trouble arises and things look bad, there is always one individual who perceives a solution and is willing to take command. Very often, that person is crazy.

—DAVE BARRY

NON SEQUITUR   By Wiley

Accept him whose faith is weak, without passing judgment on disputable matters. (Romans 14:1)

Laughter Bubblin' Up from the Boiler Room

Thelma's gem: *In Christ, "bee" the best you can "bee." . . . God will make a way.*

thelma Wells was born in 1941 in the back room of her grandparents' humble Dallas home. Her disabled, unmarried mother, Dorothy Nell Morris, was seventeen years old when Thelma was born. Crippled by a stroke soon after her own birth, the young woman had been paralyzed on one side for virtually her entire life. Despite her disability, however, the young woman insisted on her independence. After Thelma's birth, she left her parents' house and moved into the servants quarters at the home of the wealthy family she worked for, taking her baby with her.

When Thelma was two, she became very ill, and her great-grandmother, who worked as a domestic, offered to keep her until she was well. Suffering poor health herself, Thelma's mother left her at the great-grandparents' garage apartment one day and permanently ended her own mothering responsibilities. From then on, Thelma was reared in the loving and disciplined home of "Granny and Daddy Harrell," although occasionally her great-grandmother would take her to visit her mother for a few days. The most memorable visits occurred when Thelma's mother was reduced to living in a small tent she had set up on a corner of Starks Street in Dallas. Little Thelma would sleep with her mother on a narrow cot, longing for the comfort and security of Granny Harrell's house.

Even though he was blind, Daddy Harrell, Thelma's great-grandfather, was Thelma's babysitter while his wife worked. When Thelma got old enough to learn her way around the neighborhood, she led her great-grandfather to all the places they needed to go: to the fish market, the dime store, the doctor's office, to visit friends, and to church on Sundays. Together they played "prayer meeting" in the living room of their little apartment, enthusiastically belting out songs, prayers, and fire-and-brimstone sermons at the top of their lungs.

Love and Security in a Hostile World

Thelma grew up in a segregated section of Dallas, an island of love and security in an otherwise hostile world. She was nine years old, walking down one of the neighborhood streets, when a big, shiny Cadillac stopped beside her. The driver called to her, "Hey, little girl! Come here!"

Just as Thelma obediently took a step toward the car, a woman who worked in the dentist's office across the street came flying out the door, shrieking angrily, "You get yourself away from here, girl! And don't you ever let me see you hangin' on this car or talkin' to this man, understand? You don't get in anybody's car, you understand me, girl?"

As Thelma stuttered a nervous, "Yes ma'am," the woman turned her attention to the man driving the car. "And don't you ever let me catch you talkin' to this girl again!" she said in a voice that echoed down the street. "You don't want to find out what I'll do to you if I ever see you around here again!"

When the car had driven off and the woman had calmed down enough to speak in a normal voice, she bent down to look into Thelma's nine-year-old eyes. "You do what's right,

Thelma, 'cause I'll be watchin'," she warned. "And don't think I won't be talkin' to your grandmother."

The dental hygienist was just one of many guardians who kept an eye on the youngsters in Thelma's neighborhood. Later she would look back on her growing-up years and realize, "My life was being lived in front of a community that valued its children. . . . Within my small, close-knit community . . . the message was articulated clearly: 'You're a part of us, Thelma.'"[1]

Her loving, nurturing family included her paternal grand-mother, "Mother Sophie," who adored Thelma. Vivacious, flamboyant Sophie worked as a domestic but also turned her two-story home into a boardinghouse to supplement her income. It was an entrepreneurial spirit Thelma would some-day find within herself, as well.

There was one hurtful exception in this loving family and nurturing community. Thelma's maternal grandmother, "Mother Dot," was a proud and self-centered woman who was embarrassed to have a crippled daughter and, even worse, an illegitimate granddaughter. One of the causes of her resentment was that Mother Dot was a light-colored African-American while her granddaughter had very dark skin. As Thelma explained, "Because the white community treated light-skinned blacks better than those with very dark skin, it was not unusual for light-skinned Negroes to consider them-selves superior to those with darker skin. Mother Dot, with her gold-toned skin, needed no convincing to believe that her dark black . . . grandchild was an inferior creature."

Singing in the Coat Closet

On the days when Daddy Harrell couldn't baby-sit Thelma, she was taken to the home of Mother Dot, an introverted woman who had little love for her granddaughter. On the good days, Thelma was allowed to accompany Mother Dot's hus-band (Thelma's maternal grandfather), "Daddy Lawrence," as he headed off to work on the Katy Railroad streetcars. On the bad days, after Daddy Lawrence left the house, Mother Dot locked little Thelma in a narrow coat closet.

It's hard to imagine such cruelty coming from a child's own grandmother, but Mother Dot justified her actions by telling herself she was protecting Thelma. She took in ironing for a living, and she would say to Thelma as she herded her into the closet, "I don't need you gettin' burned by this hot iron."

Little Thelma would huddle in the corner of the dark closet, clutching her knees and singing to herself the gospel hymns her great-grandmother had taught her, the same hymns she and Daddy Harrell sang so delightedly when they played church. Finally she would sleep. Thus the day would pass, and then, shortly before Daddy Lawrence was due home from work, Mother Dot would open the closet door and let Thelma come out.

God Will Make a Way

There would be other hurtful experiences whenever Thelma ventured out of her neighborhood. If they were away from home all day and needed to buy a hamburger, they had to go to the back door of restaurants, standing beside the garbage cans to wait for their food. Sometimes Daddy Lawrence took her to Saturday matinees at the Majestic movie theater. They bought their tickets at a window marked "Colored Only" then entered a side door around the corner and down the alley from the grand, street-front entrance. They bought popcorn at a "Colored Only" concession stand, and they had only one choice of seats: in the balcony, with the other non-whites. Sometimes, if the balcony movie-watchers laughed too loudly, the white patrons seated below them would shout, "Shut up, niggers!"

It was just a hint of the bigotry Thelma would face when she ventured alone into the future. She finished third in her high-school class, and on the day after her graduation in 1959, she called a Dallas secretarial school to register for classes. She was told she would have to enroll in person, but when she appeared in the registrar's office, she was greeted by an indignant man who snarled, "What are *you* doing here? . . . We don't accept niggers in this school."

She returned home in tears, crushed by the man's blind hatred. Granny held Thelma in her arms, soothing her broken heart and reminding her of how much she was loved. Then she held Thelma at arm's length and said, rather indignantly, "Thelma, I thought you always wanted to go to college, not secretarial school."

Thelma reminded her great-grandmother that they had no money for college. She had hoped to get into secretarial school because it cost a lot less.

"If you want to go to college, God will make a way," Granny Harrell promised.

And He did—with help from Granny Harrell and her kind and generous employer. The Dallas aristocrat agreed to pay for Thelma's tuition and books, and almost before she knew it, Thelma was attending North Texas State College in Denton. There, only one, five-person room was available to black students in the women's dormitory. It was next to the boiler room, un-air-conditioned and filled with the ear-splitting sounds of the ancient plumbing that clanged and banged whenever the hot water was turned on anywhere in the building. That single, on-campus room was already filled during Thelma's freshman year, so she boarded with a family who lived "across the tracks" and several blocks away from the college. Later she would share the little boiler-room cubbyhole with four other girls.

The college might have called itself integrated after admitting several black students, but the campus itself was strictly segregated. Social and honorary organizations denied membership to blacks. And some of Thelma's instructors showed nothing but contempt for their black students. One of those teachers totally ignored her, even refusing to say Thelma's name when she called the class roll and never calling on her despite Thelma's eagerness to participate. When Thelma tried to speak to her after class, the instructor would leave the room or walk past her without ever acknowledging her presence. This went on for two semesters, and when the grades were posted after that last class and Thelma saw her B, she cornered the woman in her office and told her, "Mrs. Word, I just wanted to tell you that I learned a lot in your class."

The woman merely glanced up at Thelma then returned to her work without speaking.

"You're a very good teacher, and even though you didn't *want* to teach me anything, I learned a lot from you. . . . I just wanted you to know that," Thelma persisted.

Mrs. Word never looked up. But finally, she spoke. "I'm from Mississippi," she said in a slow, deliberate drawl. "I've never taught a Negress, and I don't intend to start now."

Despite the woman's hurtful words, Thelma couldn't help but smile in response. "I hate to disappoint you, Mrs. Word," she said, "but whether you wanted to or not, you did just that."

Climbing Up the Ladder

In April 1961 Thelma married George Wells, her high-school sweetheart since she was fourteen years old. George was a country boy who had moved to Dallas to work as an elevator operator in Mobil Oil's downtown office building for sixty dollars a week. They met at church, and their courtship continued throughout Thelma's high school and first two college years. Before he married her at the end of her sophomore year, George promised Granny Harrell that he would assume the costs of Thelma's college expenses and make sure she finished—and he did. Thelma graduated from college in August 1963, the same month their first child, Vickie, was one year old. In the meantime, George's job had ended when the Mobil building elevators were automated, but he and a partner had bought a Mobil franchise and had opened a service station of their own.

Thelma had a college degree, but her career in the corporate world started in the basement—literally. She thought she was being hired as a corporate secretary, but when she reported for work the first day, she was sent to the mailroom. She was the first black person the company had ever hired. "I understood from the start that my job was not simply to perform office tasks. . . . Certainly much more was required,"

Thelma said. "As a 'token,' I would fulfill the mandates of the law [requiring companies to integrate], but I would also be responsible for doing everything I could to change the perceptions and the biases of the people with whom I worked. It was up to me . . . to represent African-Americans in such a way that negative stereotypes could be broken down and ignorant prejudices could be corrected."

Instead of raising a fuss about being demoted before she ever started, Thelma vowed to be the best mail clerk she could be. That was her constant reminder to herself in that first job and in later jobs as she fought her way up the corporate ladder: "In Christ, be the best you can be."

One day, attending church, she happened to wear a gold bee pinned to the lapel of her suit. A friend complimented her on the bee and then said the words that would give Thelma the symbol that would represent her attitude from that day forward. "That sure is a pretty bee," the friend said. "Every time you wear it, remember that you can 'be-e-e' the best at whatever you want to 'be-e-e.'"

Baby Girl Morris

Thelma and George had two more children, and Thelma went on to develop her own speaking and seminar business, which became so successful that her husband and one of her daughters, a lawyer, eventually joined the company. Invitations for Thelma to share her motivational message and her diversity training poured in from around the country—and then came the overseas assignments. Thelma's first trip abroad required her to have a passport, of course. And it was then, when she was a successful executive with her own thriving business, that she first saw her birth certificate.

Her initial search of state records had been frustrating. While Thelma's parents had never married, she had known her father, Robert Smith, and had always been told her name was Thelma Smith. But no record existed for the birth of a child by that name. Instead, after a frustrating and confusing search, Thelma's birth certificate was found. The handwritten name on the document was simply "Baby Girl Morris." As far as the state of Texas was concerned, that was Thelma's legal name. Only after she went to court to change it from Baby Girl Morris to Thelma Wells could she apply for a passport.

What an incredible life Thelma Wells has lived, what fabulous goals she has accomplished since her seventeen-year-old mother scribbled those words on the name line of that birth certificate! Thelma has known adoring love and bigoted hatred, dark closets and huge arenas filled with raptly listening audiences. She has survived financial worries and health complications. She has come from a background of limitations and barriers, yet today she shares an enthusiastic message to encourage thousands of others to achieve their potential, to persevere, and to find joy through Jesus Christ.

"Nobody Told That Fool It Can't Fly"

What a blessing and inspiration it has been for me to get to know Thelma as both of us have traveled the country the last few years on the Women of Faith tour. With her steadfastly peaceful demeanor, Thelma is surely the most beloved speaker on the team. Nothing ruffles her; she is unflappable. Quick to laugh, always ready to comfort, and willing to take on any challenge presented, Thelma sometimes seems like "the only Christian on the team," Luci Swindoll quips.

And everywhere Thelma goes she wears that bumblebee. Today it's encrusted with diamonds.

Like Thelma, the bumblebee seems an unlikely prospect for success. Its body is too big; its wingspan too short. "But," as Thelma loves to say, "nobody told that fool it can't fly!" Not knowing any better, the bumblebee happily soars through every day. And so does Thelma. She sees her life as being symbolized by the bumblebee. But to me, she's nothing less than a diamond.

A Diamond in the Darkness

Have you ever seen a picture of the rock or soil where diamonds are found? It's nothing! If you're not a trained geologist, there's no way you could look at that land and suspect that it contains Earth's most valuable jewels. The pictures I've seen show a type of rock called a "conglomerate matrix." It's just a chunk of black-and-brown *nothing* with a dusty, rust-colored coating. And then an expert points to something within the rock, a tiny little grain of something you would never have noticed without help: the diamond.

Thelma came from a background with a *nothing* potential. If you had been there that day she was born in the back room of that little house in a black neighborhood in Dallas . . . if you had seen her disabled, unwed, seventeen-year-old mother scribble "Baby Girl Morris" on that birth certificate . . . you could not have suspected that this baby girl was actually a diamond in the rough. You could not have known that the little girl singing hymns in a dark, love-forsaken closet would someday sing and speak in auditoriums around the world, bringing motivation and hope to lives that had lost their spark. You could not have dreamed that this college girl, crowded with four other students into a cubbyhole next to the boiler room, would grow up to be a role model for others who would follow her courageous path through the civil rights movement, patiently enduring hatred and prejudice along the way to owning her own business. You could not have imagined that this granddaughter of domestic servants would grow up to demonstrate Christian servanthood to thousands of women across the nation as part of the largest Christian women's speaking tour in history.

You surely could not have imagined any of this . . . until you met Thelma. And then you would understand how this godly woman could turn such trials into triumph. Like a diamond, Thelma has *fire*. She sparkles in the Light of God's Word.

And like a diamond, she's *hard*. The little book of *Bible Jewels* explains it with these 134-year-old words: "You may get the hardest file that can be made and rub it on the diamond till the file is worn as smooth as glass; but it won't hurt the diamond the least in the world. It will bear a great deal of rough handling without being scratched or injured at all."[2]

Like a diamond, Thelma has borne trials and hard treatment, yet she has not let those hardships hurt her.

On the other hand, Thelma, like a diamond, "can make marks that cannot be rubbed out." In the same way that humans can use diamonds to write their names on glass, God uses Thelma to write His name across the hearts of those she meets. And nothing can erase that imprint.

And then there is that most identifying characteristic. Thelma, like a diamond, takes the Light that shines down on her and sends it out to others with the most brilliant sparkle. She flashes in the light of God's love and then sends those bright and beautiful Sonbeams outward to others.

The diamond is the birthstone for April, and it's said to represent innocence and strength. Those two attributes appear in abundance in Thelma's story. From her sheltered, loving background she emerged, sweet and innocent, into a harsh world, where she grew in strength and wisdom to become one of God's most precious jewels.

Scientists aren't exactly sure how a black piece of carbon is transformed into a dazzling diamond, but they *are* sure that tremendous heat and pressure are involved. Recently I read somewhere that diamonds are very good conductors of heat; they don't hold their temperature. This characteristic makes it easy to tell a cheap, glass imitation from a genuine diamond. The fake stone, which holds its temperature, feels warm; but the diamond is cool, having allowed any heat to pass on through it without being retained. That's what Thelma has done as the heat of hatred and bigotry has pressed down upon her life. She has let the trials turn her into a diamond, one of God's most precious jewels, without retaining any harshness that would make her bitter.

Laughing Through the Tears

One of the things I love most about Thelma is her deep, bubbly laugh. Here are some jokes and stories I've enjoyed sharing with her:

An elderly woman decided to have her portrait painted. She told the artist, "Paint me with diamond earrings, a diamond necklace, emerald bracelets, a ruby broach, and a gold Rolex watch."

"But you're not wearing any of those things," the artist argued.

"I know," she answered. "It's in case I should die before my husband. I'm sure he will remarry right away, and I want his new wife to go crazy looking for the jewelry."

Courage is the art of being the only one who knows you're scared to death.

—EARL WILSON

They keep telling us to get in touch with our bodies. Mine isn't all that communicative, but I heard from it the other day after I said, "Body, how would you like to go to the 6 A.M. class in vigorous toning?" Clear as a bell my body answered, "Listen, bozo . . . do it and die!"

SIX CHIX

Reprinted with special permission of King Features Syndicate.

A recent news report said the typical symptoms of stress are eating too much, impulse buying, and driving too fast. Are they kidding? That's my idea of a perfect day!

The only time the world beats a path to my door . . .
is when I'm in the bathroom!

RALPH By Wayne Stayskal

"I hope those people moving in across the street aren't the nosy type."

Do not be anxious about anything, but in everything, by prayer and petition, with thanksgiving, present your requests to God. And the peace of God, which transcends all understanding, will guard your hearts and your minds in Christ Jesus. (Philippians 4:6)

A Quiet Missionary
in Our Midst

Susan's gem: *I must forgive everyone. I have to maintain the character of Jesus Christ. The situations I've been in have built character into me. I have more of Jesus in me than ever because of what has happened to me. Maintaining the love of Christ and sharing it with others is what I live for.*

Susan Riley is a missionary, even though her official job title no longer contains that word and it's been years since she's seen a jungle or slept in her car while crossing the mountains in Central America. In the years since she traveled back and forth between the United States and the remotest parts of Third World nations to serve up God's Word, her life has also undergone tremendous swings between joy and misery. But she's still working in ministry, now in a new, unexpected way that sends her out into the world to touch ordinary, middle-class lives of those who desperately need to hear God's comforting, encouraging message. Maybe you've even met her and benefited from her gentle ministry without realizing what a precious jewel she is.

Today Susan travels to cities around the United States, working in marketing for a growing corporation. In her job she hosts group luncheons and other gatherings so that she can introduce her organization. She doesn't tell her own remarkable story as she chats and visits with these prospective customers. She speaks mostly of her products and programs, and, when the listener asks, she affirms her beliefs—but she doesn't mention her personal life. If she did, the tears might come. Instead, she maintains a high level of professionalism. But in every city she visits, she's come to expect something special to happen. Somehow, somewhere, without even knowing her story, a woman—or several women—are drawn to her, put before her by God's hand, as she sees it. In the faces of these women . . . in the bruises that peak out from beneath a sleeve or the dark blotches under the makeup or the eyes that suddenly fill with tears for no apparent reason . . . she sometimes sees herself a few years ago. In the veiled way the women describe their home life and in the sharp, silent hurt that fills their eyes as they speak, she reads the familiar code. And she opens her heart and encourages them with God's promises. In doing so, she has turned misery into ministry.

Following God's Call

Susan was reared in a godly home, and in her twenties, she married a Christian man who shared her zeal for doing God's work. Soon they had a very fruitful ministry and a thriving church. But they felt God calling them to the mission field, and after a few years they made the decision to follow that call.

"We had two children and a nice home, but we decided to sell everything to go to the mission field. We started with the attic—cleaned it out and made $350 in a garage sale. Then we went through the rest of the house, room by room, selling everything. We were that confident of our calling. The only things we kept were the clothes we would need, the baby's crib, and both girls' dolls. We took the crib with us and left it there in the mission field. I'm sure they're probably using it still—probably put ten babies in it every night," Susan said.

They went by ship to the West Indies, not really knowing their specific assignment. On the way they felt God's voice telling them a man would appear to help them when they got to their destination. When their ship entered the harbor, a port-pier pilot came onboard to guide the ship to port and take the passengers through customs. The pilot turned out to be a Christian minister, and Susan and her husband had no doubt he had been sent to help them. The young man served as their translator and helped them secure an auditorium where they conducted worship services that amazed even Susan and her husband with the miraculous healings and conversions that occurred. They baptized the new Christians at the seashore.

They were appalled by the living conditions they saw. "We didn't know what 'dirt poor' meant until we went to the mission field," Susan said. "And we were just as poor as those we were ministering to. Sometimes we fasted—not by choice but because there simply was no food."

The family returned to the States to raise more funds and resume a "normal" life. But they returned to their adopted country seven more times over a ten-year period. They were there when Susan was pregnant with her third child. She was already in her eighth month by the time they returned to the States and she could finally see an obstetrician. And once again God put the right man in front of her. "I only had enough money to pay his deposit—$175," Susan said. "He talked to me quite a while since I hadn't seen a doctor. He wanted to make sure I was going to be all right. But after he examined me and said I was fine, he wanted to know about our mission trip. At the end of my story, he said, 'You owe me no money. The deposit will be returned to you.' I hadn't known this doctor, but it turned out he had had a recent heart attack, and he was eager to know about the Lord. So we both got a very important gift that day." One month later, God gave Susan and her husband a healthy baby boy.

"Give Me Those Glasses"

After their last mission trip, Susan and her husband settled into an American church in the South, where he began a prosperous ministry. But as the church grew, her husband evolved into a prideful, controlling man—not only over his church but toward his family as well. Soon his once-thriving congregation took on the characteristics of a cult, and members started fleeing. Susan wished she could flee, too. "I would cry at night and ask God to deliver me from the control of this man who had become so evil, so . . . everything bad. He began degrading me in the church, calling me names, belittling anything I said or did."

But the worst abuse came *after* church. "He had always had a temper, and he had begun hitting and abusing me even while we were in the West Indies. When we were back in the States, the temper tantrums and the beatings got worse. One night he broke his hand when he hit me so hard. Another time we were away from home, attending a conference, and he beat me in the hotel room so that I went to the conference the next day with two black eyes. I tried my best to cover it up with makeup and eye shadow. Usually after he had beaten me, he would cry out, 'Oh no! You're bruised!' And sometimes that would agitate him even more."

Only once does she remember someone asking her, "Susan, where did you get that bruise?" in a way that made her think the person suspected her husband was beating her. "I told no one. I knew if I did, if people believed me, my husband would lose his job and then we would be homeless—and no doubt there would be more beatings. I had given my life to God, and I believed God's Word told me I had to stay with him; I thought I had no other choice. Besides that, I had three small children, and I thought I had no way to support them. I was terrified," she said.

Each beating would begin with the same horrifying phrase. "He would say, 'Give me those glasses,' and that was my clue. He didn't want to break my glasses when he beat me and then have to buy me a new pair."

Then one day, Susan heard evangelist Pat Robertson say on a television broadcast, "If a man beats his wife, he has already divorced her."

"Up until that moment I thought I *had* to stay with my husband, that I had no options. But then I realized the truth of what Pat Robertson was saying. I began hearing God telling me, as He did the beggar beside the Pool of Bethesda, 'Take up your bed and walk.' Word by word, God's promises delivered me. I took my children and left."

She told her husband she had been called to her own ministry. "I didn't say I was running away from him. He knew the calling I had always felt on my life, and he knew he couldn't stop that calling. So, after eighteen years of marriage, one day I simply gathered the children and fled. I left everything behind except our birth certificates and their homeschooling curriculum and supplies. The children and I ended up living in a Christian mission that had a school I could teach in. We lived in the rooms above the school."

In those difficult times, Susan felt God's voice telling her that her husband had become like Saul, distant from God, and that she and her children would never see him again. In nearly fifteen years, that prophecy has proved true. "He has never tried to contact us," she said.

A New Beginning
Eventually the divorce was finalized, and after a while God brought another man into Susan's life, Peter. They married and ministered together to Native Americans out west, even starting a Christian school in one settlement. Without a word of dissent from her first husband, Peter adopted Susan's children. At last she felt whole again, that God had sent a provider and a nurturer for her and her children. But there was something else—a yearning. Susan kept feeling a calling to return to the foreign mission field, and soon she took a trip alone to Central America. A church in the country she was visiting provided a translator, a young woman doctor. "That trip was so biblical. A little servant girl met us at

the village gate, and when we announced who we were, she ran back to tell the pastor. He was crying when he came out. He was this big, robust Spanish guy, and very friendly, but we couldn't imagine why he was crying. He said, 'My sister, I was praying in the church at five this morning and heard God say, "I am sending you a missionary from North America *today.*"' He was crying because he hadn't believed God. Later, when I got to know him, I teased him that what he really didn't believe was that the missionary God sent wasn't a man!"

The pastor told Susan he wanted to begin a Christian school on some property he owned. Susan, an accredited homeschool resources representative, promised to help. She returned home and began raising funds and gathering supplies. A year later she and her husband packed up the children and *drove* to Guatemala, an adventure in itself. They stayed three months, until the funds ran out, and helped get the school going. Today that school has two hundred students!

Susan and her family headed back for the States, praying all the way north. They weren't even sure where to go, because once again they had sold everything to go to the mission field. They eventually settled in the area where two of the three children would attend college. The third child, their oldest . . . well, that's another story.

When the family was living out west, before the trips to Guatemala, Susan's oldest child, Cathy, had had a boyfriend Susan and her husband didn't approve of. They refused to let Cathy date him, but the issue didn't seem like a major problem. Cathy had been accepted at a well-known Christian college in the Midwest and seemed excited about enrolling.

Then, on the evening of Mother's Day, when Susan had been invited to give the message at the church for Native Americans, Cathy complained of a backache. The rest of the family was going to the church to hear Susan's message, but Susan told Cathy, "You stay home, Honey. We'll be back soon."

When they returned home, Susan had a feeling something was wrong as they pulled into the driveway. Peter entered the

house and came out with a look on his face that terrified
Susan. "I really thought he had gone in there and found
Cathy dead," she said. Instead, he gently took her hand and
led her to the note left in Susan's bedroom: "Mom, don't
worry about me. I'm fine." Cathy had run away.

Susan was devastated and completely blindsided. They
searched desperately for Cathy, but she and the boyfriend
were gone. Since that heartbreaking Mother's Day evening
nearly thirteen years ago, she has seen her daughter only
twice. Once she managed to track her down to some apart-
ments out west. "Cathy opened the door, and she let me see
her baby. He was about eight weeks old. Her husband wasn't
there, but she only let me stay a few minutes. I said, 'Oh,
Cathy, I want to buy some things for the baby.' So I did that,
and I returned the next day, a Wednesday, and brought the
younger two children with me. But Cathy wouldn't open the
door. We were all heartbroken. She had told me she would go
with me to a mission conference on Sunday. That morning I
stopped at the apartment again. Cathy cracked the door open
a couple of inches and said she couldn't go."

"I Saw Fear on Her Face"

In that brief moment when Susan glimpsed her daughter's
face, she saw an emotion that she knew intimately. "I knew
her husband was on the other side of the door telling her she
couldn't go. And when I looked at Cathy I saw fear on her
face," she said. "I kissed her on the cheek and said, 'I love
you,' as I left."

Since then Susan has made other attempts to find and reach
out to Cathy, even hiring international locators to help. But
even when her whereabouts are known and gestures are
made, they are rebuffed. Christmas gifts have been returned,
unopened. Invitations to her siblings' weddings have gone
unanswered.

"We know only God can take care of this. As hard as it's
been, I have learned to just give it to Him and keep praying
and hoping—but to get on with my life," Susan said.

She was blessed by having a loving husband who supported her through this heartache. He had adopted the younger children and reared them as his own. While they finished college, she and Peter moved to another city to begin a new chapter in their lives. Susan took the marketing job, and Peter opened his own construction business, which soon developed a specialty of building and remodeling affordable homes for immigrant families.

"He was so thoughtful and caring. Once he told me about an immigrant couple who had moved into one of the homes and had nothing. Peter took one of his employees and went to a store and bought them what they needed to get started. He was very devoted to these people and helped them as much as he could," she said.

"How Can You Do This?"

She loved Peter and admired him for doing the Lord's work with such enthusiasm, so on that day when Susan came home in the middle of the day and found the county sheriff's business card stuck in her door, her heart stopped. "The sheriff had written on it, 'Please contact me as soon as possible,' and I thought Peter had had an accident. I was shaking so hard I could barely make the call, but I finally got through to the sheriff. He said, 'Oh, Mrs. Riley. I have divorce papers. When would be a good time to serve them?'"

Susan was dumbfounded. *Divorce?* Surely the sheriff had the wrong Mrs. Riley. She made him double-check the names and addresses. There had been no mistake. She summoned her children, needing their strength, as the sheriff returned and delivered the papers. Then the three of them watched, incredulously, as, a few hours later, Peter came home for dinner.

Susan asked, her voice trembling, "Peter, did you send the sheriff here today?"

"No."

"Well, divorce papers were served to me today by the sheriff."

"Oh, I thought a constable would do that," he said nonchalantly as he prepared himself a sandwich and sat at the kitchen table to eat it.

Susan's son stood at the table and asked him, "How can you do this? I am your son. I bear your name!"

But Peter didn't reply. He walked into the bedroom, packed his bags, and left. Susan was paralyzed, unable to move or speak except to say, "Peter, you know divorce is terrible."

"Yes," he said, "I know." And then her husband of twelve years left.

Later, Peter married one of the young immigrant women from the neighborhood he had helped develop.

Susan endured unimaginable pain during those dark days of abandonment and betrayal. But rather than dwell on her misery, she intensified her ministry. She never complains about what has happened to her; nor is she one who gets mired in a cesspool of self-pity. In fact, until now, she has not told her full story to anyone outside the family. Even her coworkers don't know the depth of the trials she has known—and triumphed over. It was her younger daughter who, full of love and admiration, suggested she share it here with readers of this book. "Mom, it's time," she told Susan. "Women are hurting. They need to hear this."

Thriving in Love Amid Heartache

You see, Susan didn't just survive these ordeals. She has continued to thrive in God's love despite the hardships that beset her. In her national marketing job, which sends her from coast to coast to meet with people from all sorts of backgrounds, she gently models her beliefs and shares her commitment to the gospel. "Going through these painful situations has pressed me further into the kingdom of God. I haven't wanted to go through any of these ordeals. But I know that God has used each painful crisis for good. Sometimes now I look back and think it was all some kind of dream. I've never asked, 'Why did this happen?' I've just said, 'Because of Jesus.' I know I am stronger for it, and I will continue on as a much stronger person in God than I could have been before. My focus remains on Him—and on showing Him to others by the way I live my life."

Through all of this, Susan has learned that she cannot accuse anyone. "I must forgive everyone. I have to maintain the character of Jesus Christ. The situations I've been in have built character into me. I have more of Jesus in me than ever because of what has happened to me. Maintaining the love of Christ and sharing it with others is what I live for."

As a result, hurting, struggling women are invisibly drawn to Susan, recognizing her stature as a woman of God. She eagerly welcomes them to share the hope and the love of Jesus that fill her heart. "Even before Peter left, I had women—hurting, abused wives—calling me from all over the United States," Susan said. "They had remembered me from earlier times when I was speaking in churches and working in mission fields here and abroad." Her daughter tells her, "Mom, you're a preacher and a teacher," and she does not disagree.

Sometimes the women who have casually met her or who have heard her speak in their churches really have to work hard to find Susan again, but the ones who need her most doggedly seek her out. "They trust me as one who obviously feels God's hand on my life," she said. "They have told me they consider me a mentor to them, and I cherish that role. I teach and encourage them from God's Word without telling them what has happened to me. In all this mentoring I have never told a single woman to leave her husband, but some *have* left because the abuse has been so bad."

At the luncheons and marketing meetings Susan hosts, she is no longer surprised to find herself sitting by a woman who starts out making ordinary conversation and then, a few moments later, shows a precious vulnerability by asking for Susan's spiritual encouragement and prayer to help her struggle through a troubling situation. Susan has come to expect encounters with these hurting women who need to be reminded of how powerfully God's healing touch can ease their troubled lives and how much hope they can find in His

Word. "God simply puts the women in front of me," she said. "And I am humbled to be used by Him in this way."

Sometimes women seek Susan out, remembering the ministries she shared with her last husband for twelve years; they haven't forgotten the gospel messages she delivered and the anointed way she changed lives and led unbelievers to the Lord. "Daily, someone calls me from all over the country. And when they learn that I'm now divorced, they're sad, because they remember how I ministered in their churches. They recall how I spoke out for things such as how holy matrimony is and the importance of living for God, of discipleship and of being discipled. They know how God changed their lives through Peter's and my work, and they are sad to think that joint ministry has ended," she said.

Beauty Created from Darkness

Susan's story reminds me of a beautiful slate-colored gemstone called jet. It has evolved from living material—from ancient trees that were "immersed in stagnant water millions of years ago, then compacted and fossilized by the pressures of burial."[1] Polished, it develops a beautiful luster—not cold and harsh like the harder, blacker onyx, but a soft, metallic sheen that gleams with a warm, appealing glow. While it's rarely used these days in high-fashion jewelry, in the nineteenth century, jet was cut, carved, and polished into mourning jewelry—symbolizing beauty created from darkness.

That is Susan Riley's life. Her walk with the Lord has always been a living, vibrant experience. But she has been immersed in dark, stagnant cesspools and pressured by heartache and betrayal. Even so, she has created something beautiful from the pain she has known. She has turned misery into ministry. Today she polishes her faith constantly by pressing herself further and further into the kingdom of God. As a result, her life glows in a warm, appealing way that draws others to her.

Susan could be a dull, complaining, bitter woman. Instead, she says this: "I do not look back. I look forward. I know I am in the place God wants me to be right now, because He continually puts women in front of me who need to feel His touch on their lives. Doors open constantly for me to minister."

"Reaping Where I Did Not Sow"

One of those doors took her to China last year, where, during the fiftieth anniversary of the communist revolution, she practiced prayer walking in Tiananmen Square and on the Great Wall. Susan was warned that Bibles were not allowed to be shown in public, but Susan had no fear of the government. She bravely brought out her Bible and shared several copies with people she met there. After a meeting of teachers in one Chinese city, a young college professor sought her out. "She called me late on Thursday and wanted to meet me the next day. We talked about the gospel for two hours, sitting outside, then we went to lunch. We could not close our eyes to pray, because doing so would have attracted attention that could get her in trouble. But I asked her softly, eye to eye, 'Do you want to receive this Jesus?'"

"Yes!" the woman replied.

"I had one Bible left," Susan recalled. "I started marking Scripture verses furiously to help her quickly find words of encouragement and hope. She told me, 'God has sent you to me here today so that I would make this decision.' Then we went hurrying back to her classroom, with her hanging on my arm and saying, 'I am so happy! I am so happy!'"

The college professor was the only conversion on Susan's undercover mission trip. But she is thrilled by what happened in that harsh place.

"Many times I've been on mission trips over the years, and I've been one of the pioneers, planting the seeds but being unable to see the results. In China someone else had planted the seed, and I experienced reaping where I did not sow. That teacher was so ready. And there are so many more like her there. When you look in the people's eyes, you do not see darkness. You see eagerness. They are hungry to know more. Today that woman e-mails me regularly. We converse in code, but we both know what's being said. She is brave and un-afraid, and she blesses me every time I think of her."

Laughing Through the Tears

Susan's ministry continues as she meekly serves wherever God sends her, and her tears have become precious jewels sparkling out a message of heavenly hope and Christlike love. She is a serious, no-nonsense Christian. But Susan loves to share moments of joy with all who know her. Here are some quips and quotes she's sure to like:

The world cries, "You've got to be young and you've got to be tan. You've got to be thin and you've got to be rich. You've got to be great." But Scripture says, "You don't have to be any of those things. You simply have to be yourself—at any age—as God made you, available to Him so that He can work in and through you to bring about His kingdom and His glory."

Now relax. Trust Him and be yourself!

—Luci Swindoll

Reprinted with special permission of King Features Syndicate.

The soul would have no rainbow
if the eyes had no tears.

No, I do not become discouraged. You see, God has not called me to a ministry of success. He has called me to a ministry of mercy.

—MOTHER TERESA

THE FAMILY CIRCUS.   **By Bil Keane**

Reprinted with permission of Bil Keane.

"I know what Jesus would do. He'd
ask if the shirt came in white."

The LORD your God . . . will take great delight in you, he will quiet you with his love, he will rejoice over you with singing. (Zephaniah 3:17)

Unspeakable Sorrow . . . Inexhaustible Faith . . . and a Crazy Craving for Laughter

Nancy's gem: *I've learned that my own grief is eased when I can reach out with compassion to help another hurting person whose grief is sharp and fresh.*

W hen my special friend Nancy Bryson was honored with a big humanitarian award a few years ago in Torrance, California, she was introduced as someone who "decorates lives with love and service on a daily basis." The proclamation noted that Nancy "has endured terrible grief and hardship" yet continues to serve as "a role model for countless others. . . . Giving direct aid is her first help. Second is what she does to the rest of us who should be helping, reaching out to the new lepers of our time."

Nancy reminds me of aquamarine, the birthstone for the month of March—*her* birthstone, in fact. My gemstone book says almost all the beautiful, blue-green aquamarines on the market today have been "heat treated to enhance their color." They start out as green hexagonal crystals, but in order to achieve the sparkling, radiant blue color that's prized in today's culture, they must pass through the fiery heat of the furnace.

Nancy knows about that ferocious furnace of pain.

Before her recent retirement, she spent forty years working as an acute-care nurse. As part of her continuing-education requirement to maintain her nursing license, in about 1985 she completed a class that instructed medical personnel on a devastating new disease that was spreading throughout the country. In the beginning, it was ravaging the homosexual community, especially homosexual men.

"I sat there, and I listened to all that stuff about this terrible disease and how it seemed to be especially linked to the bathhouses frequented by gay men, and I thought, *This is worse than leprosy.* And I thanked God that I didn't have to be concerned about this terrible plague affecting my family," she recalled.

"Why Didn't He Tell Us?"

Nancy and her husband, Dale, had three children: a daughter, Tammy, and two sons, Brian and Kevin. The problems started in about 1986, when Brian began having problems at school.

"Brian had been seeing a counselor. One day the counselor called and asked Dale and me to come by ourselves. And somehow, during that meeting, I listened to the counselor awhile and then I just blurted out, 'He's gay, isn't he?' Poor Dale nearly fell off the sofa! I guess, somehow, the idea had gone through my mind a few times, but I never wanted to think, *Yes, it's true.* We left the office crying. I said to Dale, 'Why didn't he tell us so we could fix him?'

"Later I was sharing this with a lady friend from church whose daughter went to the same Christian school Brian had attended. I told her we were having trouble with him, that we'd been in some counseling sessions. I told her I just didn't know how to handle it, and she suggested I get a book entitled, *Where Does a Mother Go to Resign?*."

Nancy was embarrassed for anyone to know she wanted that book. And as luck would have it, the bookstore was out of it, so she had to go to the counter and ask the clerk to order it for her. Today, fifteen years later, she still has that original, tear-stained copy.

"I read it about three times through and thought, *I have to meet this lady*," she said.

Nancy called me, as so many distraught mothers do when they find out they have a homosexual child. She left a message on my answering machine, and there was something about the tone of her voice that made me return the call as soon as I got home, even though it was nearly 10 P.M. I apologized for calling so late, but I added, "I just felt like you needed to talk."

"Yes," she said, her voice trembling just a little. "Yes, I need you."

Nancy began attending Spatula's support meetings for Christian parents at the Crystal Cathedral here in Southern California, and we became friends. I loved her quick smile and her slightly offbeat sense of humor. After the meetings, I'd call her and we'd critique the session, discussing what had been helpful or what hadn't worked. One night a woman had been upset because her son was going to marry a girl whose brother was gay. The newlyweds planned to live across the street from the homosexual brother, and the woman worried how that would affect her future grandchildren. With humor and grace, Nancy spoke up to the woman, pointing out that homosexuality isn't contagious and that gay men and women are human beings who have the same fiercely loyal love for their family members as the rest of us do. It was all I could do to keep from punctuating her words with several "Amens!"

Nancy had found a support system that was helping her work through the disappointment of having a gay son. But it was about that time when she first began seeing AIDS patients in the hospital where she worked. At one point all

three of her children worked there, too, in clerical or mainte-
nance departments.

In 1986, Nancy and Dale were called home from a camping
trip because their older son, Kevin, had been admitted to the
hospital with a rare type of pneumonia. "It never occurred to
me that it was anything but pneumonia," Nancy said. "We
went to the hospital, and the doctor told us, 'We're going to
test him for HIV.' I was flabbergasted. *Kevin?* Brian was the
homosexual one. Kevin was living a normal life—at least I
thought he was. He'd been dating girls, although he was a bit
of a loner, an introspective type. I could not believe this was
happening."

It took two weeks for the test results to come back. On the
day of Kevin's doctor appointment, the doctor called and told
me, 'I think you and Dale had better come in with him.' We
sat in the waiting room, and Kevin went in alone. Then we
were called in. Kevin paced back and forth as the doctor told
us. He said, 'It's very unfortunate, but I've just shared with
Kevin that the HIV test has come back positive.' That's what
the doctor said, but my mind was racing ahead. Kevin had
just had pneumonia. As a nurse, I knew it was more than HIV;
I knew he had full-blown AIDS."

The shell-shocked parents and son left the doctor's office
and tried to pretend their world hadn't been turned upside
down. "I had to go into work that day, the three-to-eleven
shift. Dale and Kevin drove me to the hospital, and as I got
out of the car, Kevin said, 'I'm going to beat this. It's not going
to get me.'"

A Spark of Love and Hope

Nancy got to work—to a hospital where she'd worked for
years and knew dozens of people. And she said nothing to
anyone about the whirlwind that was wreaking havoc in her
heart.

About three weeks later, Kevin got very sick. He was admitted to the hospital where his mother worked. At one point,
doctors told Nancy they did not expect Kevin to survive the

weekend. But he did, and on Monday morning, Nancy called the AIDS Project in Los Angeles and said, "My son has just been diagnosed with AIDS. Is there anyone there who could talk to me?"

The office referred Nancy to a group called MAP, Mothers of AIDS Patients. It had been started by two mothers whose sons had died of AIDS in 1984. That was at the very beginning of the AIDS epidemic in the United States, and these two mothers, knowing there would be many more grieving parents in the years ahead, decided there had to be something for these families of AIDS victims. Thus they had started the support group. One of those mothers asked Nancy where Kevin was hospitalized, and then she met Nancy there. To introduce herself, the mother didn't offer a handshake. She opened her arms for a hug.

She invited Nancy to a MAP meeting. Nancy attended, and she was amazed to see at the meeting, reaching out to others to offer encouragement and compassion, the mother of a son who had died that very week. She was seeing a live demonstration of the truth found in Proverbs 11:25: As we refresh others, we ourselves are refreshed. By helping others, the woman was helping heal her own grief. It was the spark that would ignite Nancy's own work with other grieving parents, teaching them that with love, energy, and time, they *can* survive the death of a child.

"MAP was a place we could go every month and cry and scream," Nancy said.

Kevin survived and even went back to work after a few months, but his health continued to be fragile. He managed to attend his sister, Tammy's, wedding in April 1988, and on Mother's Day he and Nancy worked together at the hospital for the last time. A little more than two years after he was diagnosed, it was obvious Kevin was dying. When Kevin became bedridden, Nancy began caring for her firstborn son at home.

"I felt it was my duty to take care of him—after all, I was a nurse. But by July, working all night at the hospital and then coming home to manage Kevin's care, I'd gotten to the point where I told myself, 'Nancy, it's time for you to be only his mother and not try to be his nurse, too,'" she said. After that, she left the medical procedures for the private nurses provided by Kevin's insurance company, and she focused on being Kevin's mother.

Even Their Neighbors Didn't Know

Nancy didn't discuss Kevin's illness outside her support groups, and Dale didn't discuss it at all. "He had been in a carpool twenty-eight years, and he had a brother who worked with him every day at the airlines. One day I asked him, 'Have you told your brother? Your carpool?'"

Dale just shook his head. Even their neighbors didn't know.

During the last month of his life, though, Nancy turned Kevin's bed so that he could talk to the neighbor kids through the window. He told them he had AIDS. "During those last weeks of his life, he really opened up, and, to be honest, I heard things I didn't want to hear. But I listened and prayed. And I cried," she said.

She worried that Kevin had not prayed the acceptance prayer and invited Jesus into his heart. But one night a pastor friend talked with Kevin and told Nancy afterward, "You don't have to worry. Kevin's heart is right. You don't have to have any concerns about that."

Through this ordeal, Nancy has learned that mothers and fathers cope with their children's deaths differently. "The last night Kevin was alive, he was comatose, in and out of consciousness. Around dinnertime, I got angry. Earlier I had asked Dale, 'Have you told Kevin how much you love him?' Dale said, 'He knows how much I love him.' But I said, 'Yes, but he needs to hear it.' Then, at dinnertime, I was fuming to my brother, 'Look at him. His son is dying, and he's sitting in the living room, watching the news. How can he do that?'

"My brother said, 'Everyone's different, and everyone deals with a loved one's death differently. Dale isn't in there watching the news because he doesn't care. He's watching the news because that's the only way he can cope.'"

With his loving family gathered around him, Kevin died on October 11, 1988. He was twenty-eight.

"We did not readily share our heartache with our neighbors, and we didn't feel comfortable saying the word *AIDS* at our church," Nancy said. "We were fortunate to have had the steadfastness of close friends and family, but for the most part, it was a very private grief."

In her support groups—Spatula and MAP—Nancy was one of the first members to lose a child to AIDS. She shared her testimony often, hoping to encourage those parents of homosexual children who had been diagnosed with the dreaded disease.

"Oh, Lord, I Cannot Walk This Road Again"

One week after Kevin died, Brian tested positive for HIV.

"He told me he'd been tested, but he lied and told me it was negative," Nancy said. "He just couldn't bear to tell me the truth, not after having watched Kevin die." For a year and a half after Kevin's death, only one person—another nurse at the hospital where they worked—knew that Brian was HIV positive. Later she would tell Nancy, "How I hated knowing what you didn't know!"

For a while, Brian seemed healthy. Then he developed a racking cough. At home he would lie on the couch and sleep. People had begun commenting, "That's a terrible cough Brian's got." And finally he went to a doctor in Long Beach.

"Long Beach?" Nancy said. "I couldn't figure out why he would go ten miles away to Long Beach to see a doctor about his cough when our family physician was just around the corner."

Then one night while she was cooking dinner, Brian came home and said, "I have to go to the hospital."

"For what?" Nancy asked.

"What do you think?" Brian snapped.

"We both cried," Nancy said. "In my mind I saw a long,

long tunnel, and I said, 'Oh, Lord, I cannot walk this road again.'"

And in her mind, she heard the Lord whisper, *I'll walk the road with you, Nancy.*

As she drove Brian to the hospital, he admitted that he had tested positive for HIV more than a year earlier. "There was no way I could lay that on you and Dad after what you'd just been through with Kevin," he said.

In July 1992, Brian came home from work complaining of a severe headache. Two days later, he was diagnosed with non-Hodgkin's lymphoma. He had severe brain swelling and over the next few weeks underwent chemo and radiation. By December, the end was near.

"We put him in the hospital on a Sunday. On Tuesday he asked me, 'Mom, do I have your permission to die?'

"We had talked about everything. Brian used to lie on the bed with me in the afternoon, and we'd talk about everything. At one point he asked me if it would be okay to make a video for his friends and his nephew and Tammy. He did make the video, but I've never been able to bring myself to watch it. That night I told him, 'Yes, Honey, you do have permission to die. I don't want you to, but I can't be selfish. You have suffered so much, and you've never complained. You don't have to keep fighting, Brian. You can let go.'"

"Where's the Light?"

They brought him home from the hospital, and Paul, the same pastor friend who'd been with Kevin near the end, asked if he could come and bring Communion to Brian and the rest of the family.

"We had the Christmas tree set up, and we'd put Brian's hospital bed in the living room so he could see it. Paul read from the Bible, and we had the most beautiful Communion service, celebrating what a beautiful life Brian had lived and how he was on his way to a better place to be with his Savior. And somehow, Paul even made some little jokes. I remember that Tammy and my sister-in-law and I sat up all night with

Brian. At one point, he called out, 'Where's the light? Where's the light? I can't see it.' I told him, 'God isn't quite ready for you yet, Brian.' Morning finally came, and I opened the drapes. I laughed and told him, 'Well, Brian, here's the light—but it's not what you were expecting.'"

Brian died on December 19, 1992. "We were all right there. I told him, 'Reach out your hands, Brian, and Jesus will reach out His hands to you from the other side.'"

God Sees You Through the Sadness

Do you think you've got it rough?

Nancy Bryson has watched two sons die. And that's not all. She helped her mother cope when, after thirty-one years of marriage, her parents divorced. Then she cared for her mother in her home as she died of cancer in 1981. And just last year, Nancy herself was diagnosed with breast cancer.

If anyone has grounds for complaining, it's Nancy. Yet listen to what she says to the dozens of grieving parents she counsels:

"God gets you through it. You think, *I could never go through all that sadness*, but God sees you through. He gives you the strength. I just keep pulling on Philippians 4:13: 'I can do all things through Christ. . . .'"

When other parents hear Nancy's story, they marvel at how upbeat and happy she seems. "I always answer, 'Well, I have my moments.' But the important thing is to get on with your day, and see what you can do for someone else."

When she's counseling other mothers whose grief is fresh, she tells them, "It's not going to be easy. Be patient with yourself. Grieving takes a long time; there's no given time frame. And it's very exhausting. You'll get tired and think something's wrong, even go to the doctor. But most of the time what you need is to rest, take care of yourself—or else you could really get sick. A few months after Brian died, I just felt like I wanted to go to bed and cry. So for three nights in a row, I just went to bed early and had a good, long cry. I worked through my feelings, and I was able to get up the next morning and get on with my life. I encourage these moms to get into a support group and to keep going as best they can but to let themselves grieve, too. Some say a support group is not for them, that they don't want to hear everyone else's problems. And sometimes it's too soon. But the important thing is to get out and try to be with others when you can."

Like a raw, green, translucent aquamarine crystal, Nancy was a good-hearted, beautiful person before these tragedies broke her heart. But as she has passed through the pain and pressure of this furnace experience, she has evolved into a beautiful gem, one of God's most precious jewels.

"It *has* been hard. I often say that cancer is dreaded, but it has respectability. AIDS doesn't evoke the same compassion. My advice to those who want to help someone else—and those who are going through the experience themselves—is to reach out to people. Listen, and then pray to your understanding God."

A Love-Filled Heart, Patched and Mended

She smiles when she remembers how a friend came up to her as Brian neared death and said, "Brian is very concerned about what's going to happen to you and Dale in your marriage after he dies."

Nancy went to Brian and said, "We've been through this with Kevin, and we've been married thirty-six years, and we won't let our marriage fall apart."

Brian replied, "Mom, go easy on Dad. You know how he is sometimes."

Nancy's heart is patched and mended, held together by God's love and a craving for joy. "Through all your sorrow, God can help you find joy and happiness," she said. "I love laughter. I try to laugh every single day. It's an element that diffuses our temptation to be self-righteous. I love people. That's why I was a nurse. And I've learned that my own grief is eased when I can reach out with compassion to help another hurting person whose grief is sharp and fresh."

Laughing Through the Tears

Now, here are some bits of wit and foolishness that Nancy and I have shared. We hope they lift your spirits and dry your tears.

NON SEQUITUR By Wiley

A conscience is what hurts when all your other parts feel so good.

If ever you make a mistake of judgment,
let it be on the side of mercy.

A first-grade teacher collected well-known proverbs. She gave each kid in her class the first half of the proverb and asked him or her to come up with the rest. Here are some of the results:

- Better to be safe than . . . punch a fifth-grader.

- You can lead a horse to water but . . . how?

- You can't teach an old dog . . . math.

- A penny saved is . . . not much.

- Children should be seen and not . . . spanked or grounded.

- Laugh and the world laughs with you. Cry and . . . you have to blow your nose.

NON SEQUITUR By Wiley

May you always find three welcomes in life: in a garden during summer, at a fireside during winter, and whatever the day or season, in the kind eyes of a friend.[1]

The four stages of life:

1. You believe in Santa Claus.

2. You don't believe in Santa Claus.

3. You are Santa Claus.

4. You look like Santa Claus!

"Our light menu is the same as our regular, but
we grab your plate before you can finish."

Thank God for . . . spirit-lifting, joy-bringing, gift-giving, love-sending, heart-mending, problem-solving, laughter-sharing, soul-searching, story-telling, fun-seeking, *forever* friends!

Listening is a magnetic and strange thing, a creative force. The friends who listen to us are the ones we move toward, and we want to sit in their radius.

—KARL MENNINGER

When you speak,
remember God is one of your listeners.

My second favorite household chore is ironing. My first is hitting my head on the top bunk bed until I faint.

—ERMA BOMBECK

[Jesus said,] "If your first concern is to look after yourself, you'll never find yourself. But if you forget about yourself and look to me, you'll find both yourself and me." (Matthew 10:39 MSG)

Using That Spiritual
Get-Out-of-Guilt-Free Card

Sandy's gem: *[Now] I can basically relax and say, "God, You've gotten me through this before. I know You'll do it again." I know He will sustain me. I don't know in what form, but I know God will put people in my life who will surround me, hold my hand, and pass me the Kleenex.*

before she even knew me, Sandy Richardson disliked me—even despised me. Thirteen years ago, as she spiraled downward in a bottomless hole of clinical depression and severe bulimia, she routinely went to Christian bookstores looking for a lifeline—something that would fix her problems, or at least make her feel better.

On one of those bookstore visits, she happened to find a pink book with a silly-looking woman on the front. The title was *Stick a Geranium in Your Hat and Be Happy*, and the author was, well . . . *me*. Sandy perused the cover, flipped it over, and read the back, and then she dropped the book as though it were contaminated.

"I was TICKED!" Sandy said later. "I was hurting, and I thought, *How dare this woman make light of my pain! How dare she tell me to be happy! She has no idea how badly I hurt!* Quite honestly, I wanted to come find you and stick a geranium . . . well, not in your *hat!*"

On the outside, Sandy seemed like a woman with every-thing going for her, but on the inside, she was miserable. And when, a couple of years later, she happened to come across another of my books, she got even madder at me. That one was entitled *Pack Up Your Gloomees in a Great Big Box, Then Sit on the Lid and Laugh.* "I thought, *I don't know who that woman is, but I hate her!* I hadn't read any Barbara Johnson books, but I assumed she was just like all the others I'd read that said if you just pray more or read your Bible more or if you can just be a better Christian, everything will be fine. Basically, they said your situation is your own fault; if you were a better Christian you wouldn't have these problems."

An Unfulfilled Need for Love

Sandy believed she had tried all those things, had tried to be a perfect Christian, but still she was consumed with a life-threatening eating disorder and devastating bouts of depres-sion. And at that point in her life, she didn't just hate me, an unknown author whose book titles made her mad. She hated herself.

Like most emotional problems, Sandy's problem had deep roots. Her unfulfilled need for love began after her father died when Sandy was only three. Her mother soon remarried, and Sandy feared but loved her stepfather, who was awkward in expressing his love toward Sandy and her sister. Her parents were loving but strict, and her stepfather had an explosive temper. His moods dictated the tone of the family's daily life. Sandy often clowned and misbehaved to get attention, but of course the attention she got was negative rather than the lov-ing affection she craved. Slowly, Sandy began to believe she was no good, especially when she was spanked or even beaten for things that didn't seem bad to her. These feelings grew stronger when, during separate instances between ages nine and twelve, Sandy was inappropriately touched by other men in her family whom she trusted to protect and care for her. She believed their actions were punishment for something wrong that she had done—something, but she didn't know what. All she knew was that she must be very wicked to have caused these men to treat her so harshly.

By the time she reached adolescence she was filled with self-hatred. When her skinny, tomboyish body changed during puberty into that of an average-sized teenage girl, Sandy felt big and clumsy even though the height and weight she had gained were within normal ranges. The self-hatred led to dark feelings of depression.

When she was fourteen, she confided her worries about her weight to her mother, who promptly took her to see the family doctor, making Sandy believe that her mother agreed she had a weight problem. The doctor prescribed a thousand-calorie-a-day diet, and thus, at age fourteen, Sandy's cycle of dieting and overeating began. It would continue for the next twenty years.

Three years later, when she was seventeen, Sandy was raped. Her attacker was the manager of the store where she worked after school and on weekends. He warned her that if she told her parents about the rape, he would say they had been having consensual sex for the past six months—and that everyone would believe him rather than her. Because she had been a rebellious teenager, to say the least, Sandy knew her parents did not trust her; she knew the rapist was right about who would be believed.

Still, she felt compelled to tell her mother. When she did, her mother was shocked into silence and left the room to call the doctor. She took Sandy to his office for a painfully embarrassing examination. The doctor questioned her and prescribed a pill to keep her from getting pregnant. And that was the end of it. The police were not called. The incident wasn't mentioned again. As Sandy would later write in her book, *Soul Hunger,* "We were a private family and kept our business hidden from others. A veil of secrecy was drawn over my rape. The subject was dropped, and I felt totally abandoned and alone."[1]

Hiding Behind a Mask

Sandy had no other way to cope with her torment except to hide it behind a mask. "I felt full of despair, convinced that my character was hopelessly flawed. My life became an exercise in building and maintaining a perfect mask," she said. She thought of the bad things that had happened to her and the mysterious evil that seemed to be a part of herself as "the brown ooze"—and she resolved that it must never show.

She focused on pretending that nothing was wrong while looking for something or someone to make her feel better. "I instinctively believed that if I put on a front good enough for someone to love me, my secrets would stay hidden, and my hunger would be satisfied," she wrote.

She got married during college. It was an abusive relationship from the beginning, and it lasted only eight months. Then came Sandy's bouts of drunkenness, sexual promiscuity, and always, that vacuum, that gnawing emptiness deep inside her that she wanted so desperately to fill with love and trust.

She joined the air force, and in 1981 she married Prince Charming—an intelligent, handsome pilot. Sandy left behind the alcohol abuse and the wild times to settle down with Scott. She was a married woman now, and she promised herself she would be the perfect Christian wife to her wonderful new husband.

On the outside, they were the perfect couple. But Sandy's heart, which she longed to fill with love, was tightly bound with cords of terror. She was terrified that her husband would discover her dark past and see her for the ugly, unlovable person she believed herself to be. In response to that fear, she took refuge in the one thing she was sure would secure Scott's love and acceptance: her appearance. "It was the perfect disguise," she wrote. "As long as I looked good on the outside, he would have no reason to look beneath the surface. He wouldn't discover my ugliness, and he would always love me."

The part of her appearance that she thought she could control most effectively was her weight. "I quit eating except for two small meals a day. In two months, I dropped almost thirty pounds," she said.

Everything Had to Be Perfect

When Scott, as well as her friends and coworkers, told her how great she looked, she knew she had found the answer to her dilemma. Soon she was showing all the classic symptoms of anorexia, an eating disorder in which the victim has a distorted image of herself, believing herself to be fat when she is in fact normal weight or less. She stopped eating. Or, when she was alone, she binged, eating a refrigerator full of food in one sitting. And then she would purge—leaning over the toilet and shoving a finger down her throat to make herself vomit.

If you only looked on the surface of her life, Sandy had achieved her goal. She had become the perfect wife. And within a few years she became the perfect mother, too, as their two daughters were born and reared with love and devotion. Life was good—if you didn't notice that Sandy excused herself after every meal, spent several moments in the bathroom, and then returned to her family, ashen-faced and teary-eyed. She also appeared to be the perfect homemaker. The fact was, she wouldn't even answer the door unless she was expecting someone. The thought of letting another person in if her house wasn't in perfect order terrified her.

Everything in Sandy's life had to be perfect . . . including herself.

If you listened carefully, you would recognize the signs of Sandy's insecurity in many ways. Reared in an anger-filled home, Sandy had never been taught to resolve conflicts any other way. The slightest difference of opinion might provoke her to rebellion, shouting, screaming, or even hitting or throwing a tantrum. There were times when she and Scott argued in the car and Sandy ended up jumping out and walking home as Scott drove slowly beside her. Any remark that she heard as criticism could set off a tantrum. "In my mind, criticism and love could not coexist," she said. "For nine years of our marriage, Scott walked on eggshells around me while I heard reproach in everything he said," Sandy wrote. "I didn't fight fair. I learned to resolve conflict by shouting, crying, and sometimes hitting. . . . I lived as an adult and spoke with an adult voice; but emotionally I was still a child."

The vicious cycle of constantly craving love and of binging and purging had engulfed Sandy in a death spiral. "I was so skinny that when I stood with my legs together my thighs didn't touch. My collarbones stuck out, and my ribs showed," she said.

"Food Became My Best Friend . . . and Worst Enemy"

Here's how Sandy described a typical binge-purge cycle that began with a few tortilla chips and salsa. "Then I would think of the ice cream I had bought and have several bowls of that. The strawberry yogurt that I got for the kids was next. . . . Then I devoured cookies until I was stuffed to the point of pain," she said. "For a brief moment, I would feel relaxed and numb."

Then the urge came to "get all those calories out of my body. Fat was not an option for me. With a stomach so full that my ribs hurt . . . I would make [my] way down the hall to the bathroom and begin the ritual.

"First, close and lock the master bedroom door. Close and lock the bathroom door. Turn on the faucet and fan to cover my noise. It was then necessary to pull back my hair to keep it clean and drape a towel over my clothes to protect them from the inevitable splatters. Leaning over the toilet, I pushed my finger as far down my throat as it would go.

"After throwing up until my stomach was empty and aching, I'd feel relief. Eyes streaming, I would wash my face, brush my teeth, and comb my hair. Next the toilet, floors, and walls needed to be scrupulously cleaned to remove any evidence. Carefully wiping up with the spray bottle of disinfectant and paper towels kept under the sink for that purpose, I would be glad that I had papered the walls with easy-to-clean vinyl wallpaper. Last, I drank a huge glass of cold water so my stomach wouldn't feel too empty.

"Then, although my stomach cramped and my throat stung, I felt better. The food was gone, and so was the fear of getting fat. I had a rush of energy and tried to ignore the guilt and remorse. How could I have done it again? Every single day I prayed that today I could stop. God knew I failed, seeing me fall short of perfection every time. In Jeremiah 23:24, God's Word tells us that He is everywhere: 'Can anyone hide in secret places so that I cannot see him? . . . Do I not fill heaven and earth?'

"My perfect manicure was marred, and my knuckles were scraped from my forced vomiting. I tried very hard not to look at my hands since they reminded me of my sin. I couldn't hide my bulimia from God, but if I was very careful I could hide it from others. No one knew, or even suspected, and I had to keep it that way. . . . Food became my best friend and worst enemy. I wanted food, looked forward to eating it, even dreamed about it—and regretted every bite I ate."

Sandy and Scott had been married nine years and their older daughter was nearing kindergarten age when Sandy happened upon a full-page magazine advertisement that said, "We can help women suffering from anorexia and bulimia. . . . Our Christ-centered approach allows each guest to build the confidence to deal with the problems and stresses of everyday life without starving, binging, or purging."

She was stunned. "I knew that what I was doing had a name, but I had no idea that there were enough women like me to warrant a hospital."

When Sandy dialed the number for Remuda, the cords that had bound her heart for so long slowly began to loosen. Relieved to hear that insurance would cover most of the cost, Sandy hung up, realizing that the counselor had already given her the first tool for fighting her way out of her emotional prison. The stranger on the other end of the line had given her hope.

When Scott came home that night, she confessed to him that throughout their marriage she had been anorexic and bulimic and now she had found a hospital where she could be treated. He was shocked . . . and angry. He had watched her grab at straws over the years in an attempt to feel better— diets, hormone therapy, vitamins, psychological therapy. Now she wanted to leave him and the girls for what could be a period of *months* away from home?

But somehow she managed to pull it off. She got Scott's okay and wrangled a leave of absence from work. She was relieved to have her parents offer to help care for the girls. Within a few days she said a tearful good-bye to her husband and daughters and flew from their home in Wisconsin to Arizona.

She was surprised to find that Remuda was a ranch, not a hospital. Adobe buildings and fenced corrals full of horses surrounded the main lodge, with its rustic log interior that radiated comfort and relaxation. Stately mountains rose in the distance, and gentle pathways wove through the gently sloped landscaping. Despite the peaceful setting, it was diffi- cult for Sandy to relax those first few days, but gradually the therapy began to have an effect. In her book, *Soul Hunger,* she recalls that "nurses, therapists and mental health techs focused all day, every day, on our feelings."

The staff reassured Sandy and the other patients that "everyone has pain and trials in their lives. Healthy people face the pain and work through it. Unhealthy people lie about it, cover it up, resort to addictive behavior to dull it or deny that pain exists for them."

To Sandy, it was a new and revolutionary concept to realize "all the people I had compared myself to and considered per- fect *weren't.*" She was discovering that everyone is human and that if she asked the right questions or looked closely at their lives, she would see they had struggles of their own. The difference between mental illness and health, she learned, was "the ability to face problems head-on rather than run from them."

At Remuda, step by step, Sandy gathered information—

from personality basics to family dynamics—that gave her "a glimmer of how to put my life back together. I was learning the 'whys' of eating-disordered behavior, from its roots to its addictive components."

"God Wanted Me Well"

Sandy's book chronicles the details of her treatment and her turnaround. Just let me share here that one of the lifelines that pulled her through that process: the belief she renewed there that "God wanted me well and that Jesus had died on the cross so I might have a full, healthy life." But in the past this belief had been tempered by church doctrine that had told her if she just had enough faith then God would heal her. So she had been tormented by the question, "If it were true that I should be healed by faith alone, then was I a bad Christian because I was bulimic and depressed? . . . If my faith was inadequate, then it was my fault that I was sick. I would be healed if I had greater faith, or so I thought."

At Remuda, her therapists told her to let faith give her the courage to walk *through* the painful process of becoming whole, one step at a time. That process included forgiving others for their painful actions that had weakened Sandy emotionally and also asking God to forgive her for her own mistakes.

It wasn't easy. Sandy began that walk toward wholeness only after spending a long time in what she described as a black hole of hopelessness. In her sixth week at Remuda, Sandy finally dropped her defenses, climbed out of her hopelessness, opened her heart, and began to rebuild her life.

She returned home to her family in April, having left them in January. It would be wonderful to say that Sandy and her family "lived happily ever after" and that their life together has been a bed of roses. But that wouldn't be true. Their life to-gether has been rewarding and love-filled. But there also have been struggles and challenges. Recovery is an ongoing project for Sandy, and in the process of recovering, she has taken these three courageous steps:

- She "came clean," not only with her family but with her friends, telling them about how her eating disorder had controlled her behavior before treatment. She had been nervous about confessing her story to her friends, but she was reassured when one of them shared a favorite Scripture verse with her: "Being confident of this, that he who began a good work in you will carry it on to completion until the day of Christ Jesus" (Philippians 1:6).

- She was frightened to be challenged by some people in the Christian community who seriously questioned her wisdom in going through therapy. "They saw psychological help as a departure from Scripture, and some even questioned my faith," she wrote. These encounters were unsettling, but she kept telling herself, "God has brought me this far, and I'm not about to panic." In fact, she saw her ability to disagree without panicking as another step in her journey.

- She spoke with her pastor and his wife about her loneliness and her fear of being the only one in the church with problems. She was amazed to hear her pastor say there were *many* hurting people in their church. She was even more amazed when he invited her to share her story in the couples Sunday school class she and her husband attended.

Proving the Promise True

In the past, Sandy's life had been plagued with shame and guilt over her sordid past, her compulsive drive for perfection, her anger-filled temperament, her eating disorder, and all the other dark behaviors that made up "the brown ooze." But her Remuda therapist had given her a lifelong "get-out-of-guilt-free" card by telling her that "God is so powerful He can use *anything* to serve His purposes." And on that Sunday morning when Sandy stood, knees knocking and heart pounding, before fifty people in the Sunday school classroom with her husband, Scott, in the front row, she proved that promise true. Sandy was taking the first step toward turning her misery into ministry.

Since then, Sandy has continued to use the fractured pieces of her life to help patch up the broken hearts of others. She, Scott, and their two teenage daughters now live in Arizona, where she is the executive director of the Remuda Foundation, a nonprofit agency that exists to provide treatment awareness and prevention of eating disorders. She also finds Christian out-patient providers for Remuda clients after they go back to their homes. And she speaks at Remuda chapel sessions, both to give back what God has given her and to support the new patients.

Today, Sandy's life is rich, happy, and authentic. But that doesn't mean she hasn't had a few repeat visits to that black hole of hopelessness since she first arrived at Remuda ten years ago. In fact, she frankly admits that she's had one relapse with bulimia since then, and she even attempted suicide twice. But that "get-out-of-guilt-card" keeps coming into play, and she can easily see how God has used even those tortured events for something good.

"Why Was I So Unhappy?"

"The relapse was good, because it reminded me that I didn't know how to stop that kind of behavior before treatment, but I *did* know how to stop afterward. And I did stop. What I couldn't understand, though, was why was I so unhappy, so depressed? I felt I must be doing something wrong; otherwise I wouldn't be so unhappy. The two deep depressions when I attempted suicide taught me a lot, as well. I had a secular social worker—he had no relationship to Christ, but he understood my faith was important to me. I asked him, 'What's God trying to teach me?' and he answered so wisely, 'Maybe He's not trying to teach you anything. Maybe you have some things you need to *unlearn.*' And he was right. Another therapist helped me see that I thought I had given up control, but I hadn't. I was still trying to control all of life. My husband had to be constantly reassuring to me. And I knew I couldn't control everything about my kids, but I felt I had to control how their lives turned out. Gradually, I learned to let God have control of the outcomes of my life. Then the suicidal depressions lifted. Since then there have been some biochemical depressions, but when those come on me, I can basically relax and say, 'God, You've gotten me through this before. I know You'll do it again.' I know He will sustain me. I don't know in what form, but I know God will put people in my life who will surround me, hold my hand, and pass me the Kleenex. And because of all that's happened to me, I know He will use even that step on the journey to encourage other people."

Being the mother of two teenagers is itself a challenge. "I'm convinced that God gave us kids to keep us on our knees," she says with a laugh. She almost has a tone of pride in her voice as she describes her two daughters' distinct styles: "One of my daughters is the GAP queen—all preppy and coordinated. And my other daughter has a sense of style that sometimes frightens me. Before, I would have tried *everything* to get her to change her style. Now I know I can't control what she is, and I do all that I can to support her whenever I can. I've learned to laugh and say, 'It's only hair. So what if it's vertical?' I have a new perspective on life after all that I've been through."

Ten years ago, Sandy was Remuda's fifth client when the facility had 13 beds; now Remuda operates three ranch centers and one partial-care facility totaling 130 beds. Remuda representatives work in a booth at Women of Faith conferences, offering information about their program. It was in that capacity that Sandy Richardson heard me speak at a conference three years ago. We had never met, but the next week, she wrote me a letter, apologizing for misjudging me because of my silly book titles. "When I heard you speak at the conference, I saw your heart that day, and I loved you. Now I've *read* your books, and I recommend them to women in pain."

Afterward, I read Sandy's book. Then we happened to sit next to each other on a plane. Her story and her sincerity touched my heart, just as she has touched hundreds of others as she's worked with Remuda clients.

"I'm amazed and humbled every day at the way God uses me," she said. "And the most amazing thing is, the more real I am, the more people are drawn to that. When I'm willing to be vulnerable and let it all hang out, it gives people permission to do the same. A lot of my own struggles centered around not finding anyone to relate to. All the Christians I knew were perfect—they wouldn't even let someone see their unmade beds, let alone what was going on in their lives. But the truth is, life is tough for all of us."

What We Need When We're Scared

That vulnerability continues into Sandy's life today. "Recently someone very close to me went through an awful bout of depression, and it scared me to death. Going through that, I could have plastered a mask on my face and said, 'Oh, things are fine,' or I could say, 'Things are tough right now.' When I do that, people are warm and understanding. And that's what you need when you're scared.

"I used to 'catastrophize,' blowing minor incidents out of proportion and thinking everything was the end of the world. Now I realize God's in control. I might still do a little catastrophizing, but I then say, okay, what if the worst happens? What if someone I love dies? It'll be heartbreaking, no doubt about it. But I know that God will sustain me. It's like the verse from Job that you often quote, Barb: 'Though he slay me, yet will I trust in him.' These days, the people I admire most aren't the ones who have no problems, but the ones who bear their problems with grace and patience."

In her nationwide travels, Sandy often sees glimpses of her old self in those around her. "I'll be sitting at dinner with a group of women somewhere, and I'll see the scraped knuckles, or I'll be in the restroom at a restaurant and notice tiny splatters on the wall or floor—things other people probably wouldn't notice at all—and I'll think, *She's in here somewhere, Lord. Please help her find her way out of that black hole . . .*"

A Special Place Inside Her Heart

Sandy is a rare gem, a woman whose heart holds both agony and joy—agony from remembering how dark her life has been and joy in knowing she has helped countless others escape from that same painful prison. Her life reminds me of an emerald. Did you know emeralds are even rarer than diamonds? They are rare "because they are a mixture of elements that don't ordinarily get a chance to mix: 'They are a mineral that shouldn't exist at all,'" according to one expert.[2]

An emerald is made up of beryl with a little chromium or vanadium mixed in. The paradox is that beryl is in the chemical family considered by scientists to be the "light side," while chromium and vanadium are from the "dark side." There's no common reason for these two families of elements to be found together, but very, very rarely they are. And the result is a beautiful, sparkling emerald.

Besides their paradoxical composition, the most sought-after emeralds have another intriguing feature that reminds me of Sandy. It distinguishes an authentic emerald from a man-made fake. These highly treasured emeralds contain a microscopic pocket—usually no more than a hundredth of an inch wide. This little pocket is like the invisible emptiness Sandy felt, that place where love should have been that she kept trying to fill with food and wild behavior when she was fighting the demons of depression and bulimia. But the little pocket in the treasured emerald isn't empty. It's filled with an ancient liquid plus a tiny crystal of salt. Likewise, that special place deep inside Sandy's heart is also filled these days—with the blood of the Savior, who loved her enough to die for her, plus a tiny crystal of faith, no bigger than a mustard seed, that sends her out into our hurting world, courageously using her own tears to be the salt of the earth today.

Laughing Through the Tears

A Christian who walks by faith accepts all circumstances from God. He thanks God when everything goes good, when every-

thing goes bad, and for the "blues" somewhere in-between.
He thanks God whether he feels like it or not.

—ERWIN W. LUTZER

Persistence. If your ship doesn't come in, swim out to it!

—JONATHAN WINTERS

If you can't be a good example . . . at least you can serve as a
horrible warning.

We, as Christians, need to stop telling God how big our mountains are and start telling our mountains how big our God is!

—JOHN OSTEEN

Good friends are like stars. You can't always see them, but you know they're always there.

THE FAMILY CIRCUS ®   **By Bil Keane**

"Why is that silly man blowing his horn?"

Bumper Sticker:
If you can read this . . . I've lost my trailer.

Life is what's coming—not what was.

"You can get up now, Mr. Garner,
I'm back on the road again."

Husband to wife: "When I think of what you have meant to me all these years, it's all I can do to keep from telling you."

Members of a male club at a well-known university criticized very negatively and strictly each other's literary writings. At their meetings they tore one another's compositions to pieces.

A girls club at the same university did something similar except that they commended each other for the good points in their writings.

Not one of the men made it in the literary world, but a half-dozen of the girls became famous writers.

God comes by His Spirit and His Word and tells us how wonderful we can be by His grace. The Bible says, "It doth not yet appear what we shall be: but we know that, when he shall appear, we shall be like him" (1 John 3:2 KJV). He has a wonderful plan or blueprint for each of our lives: He calls us "his workmanship" (Ephesians 2:10 KJV). It is written about us: "They shall be mine, saith the LORD of hosts, in that day when I make up my jewels" (Malachi 3:17 KJV). We are not just creatures of the dust but God's special treasure.[3]

Want to see a miracle? Plant a word of love heartdeep in a person's life. Nurture it with a smile and a prayer, and watch what happens. . . . Sowing seeds of peace is like sowing beans. You don't know why it works; you just know it does. Seeds are planted, and topsoils of hurt are shoved away. . . . Never underestimate the power of a seed.

—MAX LUCADO

One day a father was talking to a friend about his son, who had caused great heartache. The friend said, "If he were my son, I would kick him out."

The father thought for a moment, then said, "Yes, if he were your son, so would I. But he is not your son; he is mine, and I can't do it."

God himself is right alongside to keep you steady and on track until things are all wrapped up by Jesus. . . . He will never give up on you. Never forget that. (1 Corinthians 1:8–9 MSG)

Waiting for Another Chance to Say, "I Love You"

Evelyn's gem: *My pastor and his wife know my story. . . . If someone comes to them and says, "I have this problem, . . ." my pastor knows to send those people to me. I've identified myself as someone who's willing to reach out to these parents.*

beautiful, deep blue sapphires have been valued since biblical times. Like many of the jewels described in this book, the sapphire was one of the gems designated for the Jewish high priest's breastplate of judgment in the Book of Exodus. And according to ancient Jewish traditions, when Moses descended Mount Sinai after receiving the Ten Commandments, he was carrying two slabs of sapphire on which God had etched the laws with His own finger.[1]

The sapphire has continued to be associated with the church throughout the ages. Bishops once wore sapphire rings to indicate their rank, and in olden times it was thought that wearing a sapphire over your heart would help make you strong. One of my favorite stories about this centuries-old custom of valuing sapphires says that, in the vaults of a French cathedral, there is an ancient sapphire clasp that fastened the imperial mantel over Charlemagne's body after the beloved emperor died in the year 814. According to legend, the sapphire in the clasp is truly exquisite, yet there is something else in the clasp's ornate setting that is even more valuable than the extraordinary gemstone. In the clasp's gold mounting, there is said to be a small, coarse sliver of wood: a splinter from the cross of Calvary.

The writer of the old book *Bible Jewels* equated Christian faith to this belief about sapphires' imparting strength. "Faith may be compared to the sapphire, because it makes us strong," he wrote. "Faith makes us strong to *suffer*. . . . The second reason why faith may be compared to the sapphire is because it makes us strong to *serve*."[2]

When I read that beautiful analogy, I thought immediately of my friend Evelyn Harris. She is like a deep blue sapphire because she has been strong while suffering a mother's immense heartache, and she has risen up from her own hurts to serve other mothers with love and concern. Here is her story.

Happy Times Despite Hardship

When Evelyn's son, Craig, was three years old, Evelyn discovered that her husband was sexually abusing the little boy, her only child. Taking Craig with her, Evelyn immediately left her husband and eventually finalized divorce actions against him. She knew she was doing the right thing, but the divorce left her without any means of supporting herself or her son. "This was back in the days when a single woman couldn't open a charge account or get a loan or anything like that without a great deal of difficulty," Evelyn said. She lived with her parents awhile then stumbled upon a way to be self-supporting while also staying home with her young son. She rented a home big enough to share, and she sublet rooms to other women—sometimes to women like herself with young children, and other times to girls who were attending college in the north-eastern city where she lived. She also took in ironing and cleaned houses—everything she could think of to provide enough income for her to be a stay-at-home mom.

Craig was a bright, active boy, and he and his mother became very close in their years together. Evelyn worked hard, but she always had time to spend with Craig, and whenever he wasn't in school, he was near his mother. "We had some very good times," she said, laughing at the memories. "We were happy."

There was one scary time when Craig had a vision problem that caused doctors to run brain-wave tests and other examinations. For a while the experts told Evelyn her son "wasn't developing as he should." But in the end, after four or five months of uncertainty, they said he was fine.

Then, during Craig's early teen years, Evelyn began to notice things about him that disturbed her. "The way he walked, some of the things he liked or disliked. He got a little heavy and seemed somewhat feminine, and kids sometimes made fun of him. But he dated a lot, and I felt secure about him, because I knew he'd gotten a firm grounding in the Lord. We had been faithful churchgoers, and Craig had sung in the choir and attended church camps."

Evelyn's confidence increased when Craig decided to go to a Christian college after high-school graduation. "He dieted and lost the extra weight, and he went off to college, and I thought, *God's going to take care of him,*" she said.

But things didn't work out the way Evelyn expected. Once he was enrolled in college, Craig changed his name and slipped into the homosexual lifestyle. Evelyn saw the signs whenever Craig came home, but she didn't want to believe what she was seeing. When Craig graduated from the Christian college, Evelyn flew out to the campus to attend the ceremonies. "Within twenty minutes of arriving on campus, I'd met his friends and seen the way he lived, and I was so mad at God," she said. "I thought, *He goes out here to this Christian college and look what happens.* After graduation he came back home and was very much in the lifestyle in the way he dressed and walked and in how he dealt with his life and his friends. He partied with them all the time; those homosexual friends were the main thing in his life at that point. Somehow Craig's homosexuality was all around me, but I had *not* accepted it, and we had never discussed it. He was my only child. I had invested so much of myself in him, and I couldn't believe what was happening. It broke my heart to even consider it."

On one of her darkest days, Evelyn went into a Christian bookstore, looking for help. And on a bottom shelf, her eye happened to notice a title that instantly appealed to her: *Where Does a Mother Go to Resign?* She thought, *That's exactly how I feel right now,* and she bought the book, read it in a single night, and called the author the next day. That's how Evelyn Harris and I became cross-country pals all those years ago.

"Barb, your books and tapes and gifts saved my life," she said. "Remember how we used to call each other and cry about what was going on with our kids? I still have that little music box you sent me to set in my windowsill. When the sun hits the little coil on the back, a little bird in the box sings and reminds me of you."

She gave Craig a copy of *Where Does a Mother Go to Resign?* and when he gave it back to her he said the book was "overrated. It can't be that hard to be the mother of a homosexual," he told her.

A Moment Frozen in Time

Despite this conflict brewing in their lives, Evelyn and Craig spent lots of time together and enjoyed each other's company. "We never had any money, so we did things that didn't cost a lot. Sometimes we'd splurge on a movie, but most of our activities centered around the church, because that was our life," she said. On one of their movie trips they met two girls Craig knew. Evelyn invited them back to their home for dinner. "I was in the kitchen, and he and the girls were in the other room. One of them said to him, 'How long have you known you're homosexual?' My heart stopped. I remember that moment as though it is frozen in time. It was the first time that word had been spoken aloud in our house. Craig answered casually, 'Oh, I've always known.'"

One of the hardest parts for Evelyn after that moment was dealing with her own physical reaction to Craig. "Once that word was spoken and his homosexuality was out there and acknowledged, I had a hard time letting him touch me—kiss me or hug me. I knew what went on in that lifestyle, and I had a physical reaction to it. I didn't know how to handle that problem at all. Here was my only child, this son I had adored and cherished all his life, and suddenly I didn't want to touch him."

As time went on, Craig occasionally disappeared for months at a time, and Evelyn agonized over what might be happening to him. Craig would reappear in her life and then vanish again. "There have been years when I didn't even know where he was or whether he was dead or alive," she said. "Once when we were together we were coming home from somewhere and we went by a really bad neighborhood. Craig pointed in there and said, 'That's where I lived with so-and-so [one of his gay lovers] for three months.' Then the nausea would come back, to think that my son had lived in a place like that."

Craig and Evelyn didn't talk about the Scripture verses concerning homosexuality. "He knew them so well, having been reared in church and having graduated from a Christian school. He knew homosexuality was wrong. My attitude has been that yes, he is homosexual and he probably cannot change. But he could remain celibate as many other people do. We fought over the fact that he lived that lifestyle," she said.

One year Craig fell in love with a man from their church, and the two of them set off for the South where they had heard of someone who would marry them. But they had a bitter fight along the way, and Craig soon returned home in great despair.

"At one point I went to the pastor of our church and said, 'This is my problem,'" Evelyn said.

"Yes, I know," he answered.

"This is a large church; I can't be the only one who is dealing with this," she said.

"Of course you're not," the pastor told her, "but the rest are handling it better."

Evelyn finally found a Christian counselor who helped her get her life back on track. By then she had held a job outside the home for several years, and she was still taking in college girls as boarders in her home. Craig lived in an apartment up the street and had various lovers and male friends who frequented there. Rather than condemning and ostracizing herself from her son and his friends, Evelyn mothered them all.

"I was working in a drapery shop then, and I helped Craig make curtains for the apartment. I became friends with some of his boyfriends, and they would come over to talk to me and tell me they didn't want to be gay but they couldn't help it," she said.

Sometimes Craig would become extremely distraught that a lover had broken up with him. That's when Evelyn realized there was something else going on his emotional life. Now she knows Craig suffers from a condition called dissociative disorder, which can be the result of childhood sexual abuse. The disorder causes a switching in personality. The affected person does not remember a large segment of his or her previous life or anyone connected to him or her. There is no recall of family, friends, or events, even fun times.

The Greatest Hurt

"I never really believed in things like that before I learned about Craig, but now I know it is true, and it has caused the greatest hurt to me," she said. "This is what I've really lost him to, this personality disorder. There are years now when he has no idea who I am. He can recall my name but doesn't know we are related and makes no connection to any part of our past lives together. Then, just as suddenly, he calls and, for maybe a year at most, he is here and loving and thoughtful and totally in touch with his life—although he's not able to remember the years in between these totally conscious periods. I never know when he may surface, and I know even less when the son I know will disappear again. Then he is unable to work and no one ever sees him. These two different phases of his life are represented in the mail I've received from him. I have lots of loving letters and cards from him, and then there are letters that ramble with anger and condemning scriptures telling me I will be going to hell and he will laugh."

There have been times when Craig has been so disconsolate after a breakup that he has threatened suicide. At one point, he was gone for seven years, and again Evelyn didn't know where he was or whether he was alive. And then he reappeared and, amazingly, got married.

"Someone in church came up to me and said, 'You must be really excited.' I asked, 'About what?' And she said, 'About Craig getting married and having the big wedding.' I was dumbfounded. I hadn't known anything about it," she said.

Craig and his fiancée had someone hand-deliver a wedding invitation to her. "But by the time I got it, it was already after the RSVP date. I was trying to decide whether to go when I got a letter from Craig telling me not to come and that they would have people posted at the door to keep me out. A friend offered to drive me there, and I asked Craig if I could just sit in the car outside the church and watch them come out, but he said no."

Evelyn was heartbroken. But she didn't just sit home and grieve. Since reading *Where Does a Mother Go to Resign?* she had reached out to help other moms going through problems with their children. When she contacted a local mental health agency for help, she was told there was no support group for families of dissociative disorder patients. "I told them, 'Well, if anyone else calls and asks you this question, give them my name and phone number.'"

In the same way, she has reached out to other mothers who have homosexual or mentally ill children or who are in the midst of an estrangement, as she is. She changed her membership to a church where she was encouraged to start up a parents support group similar to our Spatula support groups that operate around the country.

"In those days, years ago, men would come with their wives

but they rarely participated; they just wouldn't talk about their children who were homosexual. In fact, some parents would come from out of state to attend our meetings because they couldn't tell anyone back home. Since the group started, we've met once a month, and during that time, parents have come and gone. And some sons have died. One woman who came was very upset. She'd just learned that her son was gay and he had been asked to leave the priesthood for that reason. After a while she stopped coming, and I didn't hear from her for a while. Then one day she called and said she had started a group in the Catholic church for both men and women, and they did *lots* of talking. Barb, I laughed and called you that day and told you these were your Spatula grandchildren—an offshoot support group started by someone who had first attended a Spatula-style support group."

Someone to Call

Evelyn was also willing to let me pass on the names of mothers in her area who had contacted me for help. That led to one of our favorite stories. One day a couple came into the drapery shop where Evelyn worked and placed an order for drapes. As Evelyn cheerfully placed the order for the couple that day, the woman turned to her husband and whispered, "Now, *there's* a woman who's never had a problem in her life." Evelyn didn't hear the woman say that, but she found out about it later when I gave her the name and phone number of a mother in her area who had called me for help. Evelyn called the woman, and they enjoyed a phone chat. The other woman had *two* sons in the homosexual lifestyle and really needed another mother to talk to. Evelyn invited her to her home, and when she showed up on Evelyn's doorstep, they both realized they had seen each other somewhere before—but where?

"Finally, we figured out that I worked in the drapery shop and had placed the recent order for her," said Evelyn. "Then she told me what she had said to her husband that day, that I surely had never had a real problem in my life. We laughed and laughed about that. And it's been a real comfort to both of us to have someone to call when things get rough."

Evelyn's going through one of those rough times now. Ironically, it follows one of the happiest times of her life.

"After Craig and Vickie were married, I didn't hear from them for a long time. Then, on the day before Christmas Eve, Vickie called me. She said, 'Evelyn, I think Craig needs to see you. You two need to get these troubles ironed out.' Well, I suggested we meet in a public place, and I went out and got some gifts and met them at a restaurant, and they showed me their wedding pictures. Then we had a really good year. We talked often and had pizza together. Craig would bring his guitar sometimes and sing for me. And that next Christmas they invited me to their home to celebrate. Vickie's mother was there, and they had invited the girl who was boarding with me at the time. I can't even describe how wonderful it was. It was like a movie, a fairy tale. It was the most wonderful Christmas I can remember," Evelyn said.

"It Was Over So Fast"

On December 31, Craig and Vickie were out of town attending a New Year's Eve party, and they called Evelyn at midnight to wish her a happy New Year. A few days later, Evelyn had a doctor's appointment, and Craig had said he would take her to the clinic. But he didn't show up at the agreed-upon time. Evelyn called Vickie at work. "Uh, you'll have to check with Craig," she said.

"But I can't find him! Where is he?" Evelyn asked. Vickie didn't answer.

That night, Craig called and told his mother, "You and I are *not* family anymore. I never want to have anything to do with you ever again."

"It was over so fast," Evelyn said, remembering that painful night. "If I hadn't had a girl here living with me who had been part of it all and could vouch for it, I would have thought it was a bad dream."

That was three years ago. Since then Evelyn has seen Craig

twice in their neighborhood: once in a parking lot and another time in the grocery store. "I was in one line, and he was in another. He saw me and turned his back," she said sadly.

The pain of seeing him again deepened the ache in her broken heart. For a few days, she continually asked God, *Why?* And when the answer came, it made her smile. "It was as if God told me, 'Evelyn, you have been praying for someone to at least see Craig so you would know he is okay. I decided to let you be the one to see him because I know about you mothers. You would not have been content with a secondhand picture. Now, go do what you are to do and rest in the fact that your son is alive and well.'"

She knows that Craig's mental illness has once again taken control. She prays that he will call again, resume contact with her. But she knows that may never happen. "I've made all the arrangements in case the worst happens and I die without seeing my son again. I've donated my body to medical research, and I've written my will so that everything is taken care of."

Instead of letting her grief consume her, Evelyn has focused her life outward to help other mothers of homosexuals and especially other mothers whose loved ones are struggling with dissociative disorder. "It is such a sad way to lose your child," she said. "I have a burden for those mothers who must deal with this. There really is no Christian help for this problem out there. It seems that getting too close to buried truths somewhere within the person's past causes him or her to switch over and withdraw because those things just can't be dealt with."

Helping Each Other Find Peace

Evelyn's church friends are her family now. "I go to every church service and every activity, because I need them all," she said. "I want people in my church to see me there, worshiping the Lord, so that someday, if some of them are hurting, they'll feel they can confide in me. My pastor and his wife know my story. And I know that if someone comes to them and says, 'I have this problem, and there have to be others here,' as I did all those years ago in another church, they won't get the answer I got: 'Yes, there are others, but they're handling it better.' My pastor knows to send those people to me. I've identified myself as someone who's willing to reach out to these parents."

Recently she accepted the job of mentoring a group of women at the church. "It's simply a way of lifting up women and helping each other find the peace I have found and the encouragement I've received," she said.

In her everyday life she's continually amazed at all the mothers she's encountered who are also dealing with a heartbreaking estrangement from their children. "I've learned there are a lot of mothers out there whose children have chosen to walk out of their lives. By now I believe I can smell them! I know them when I see them. Even when they're laughing there's just something sad about them. For example, one of the women I work with was so excited, waiting for the birth of her granddaughter. Then she never mentioned it. Very quietly, I asked her about it one day, and she said for some reason her daughter and son-in-law had decided to break their relationship with her, and she hadn't seen her granddaughter. I simply told her, 'My son and I are in that same hard place.' It's too painful for her to discuss right now, but she told me, 'At least I know there's someone else who knows what it's like to have a child on the face of this earth who doesn't care whether his mother is alive or dead.'"

And then there is Evelyn's neighbor, who said to her one day, "Your son used to be around all the time, and now I never see him."

"He's not in my life anymore," Evelyn said with a sigh.

"My daughter's not in my life, either," the neighbor replied.

"So now we talk about our lost children sometimes, and it helps to know someone understands," Evelyn said. "Whenever I sense that someone has an estrangement I try to let them know that I understand, that there's someone who feels the same hurt they feel. There have been times when I've wanted to go into my backyard and bury something and have a funeral service, because something of me has died. The dreams have died. When your child is in this lifestyle you don't know where he is or whether he's dead or alive. At least when parents of AIDS victims grieve, they have a place to go, a grave to visit. When someone asks me about my son, I just say I don't know. I don't know where he is. I don't even know if he's alive."

There are these nights of sorrow in Evelyn's life. But there are equally powerful mornings full of joy. Retired now and working part-time, Evelyn relishes the work she does.

"I always make plans for the holidays that help other people," she said. "For three years I served meals on Christmas Day at a psychiatric hospital. I try to plan Christmas visits to people who might be alone, or I write letters to the mothers I know who are hurting for various reasons. It's important work to me."

Evelyn has also received a tremendous blessing from something that originally grew out of hardship. "When I started taking in these young college students as boarders as a way of supporting myself and Craig all those years ago, I had no idea what a blessing these girls would be to me. They're like the daughters I never had. Usually at least one of them will manage to stop by for Thanksgiving or Christmas, and I try to collect funny things to share with them when they come. We laugh and enjoy our time together, and you'd never know there was any pain in my life at all."

Evelyn has known tremendous sorrow. But she has also known the joy of helping others. If you are one of those mothers who finds her way to Evelyn, here is how she will share words of comfort and advice with you:

"It's hard to come to terms with the fact that so many of your hopes and dreams are gone. It's overwhelming. So I often ask, 'What hurts *most?*' Then I tell the mom there's probably nothing she feels that I haven't felt too. Sooner or later, the hardest hurt does go away. You never get over it; you never get used to it. But the hardest part eases, and you feel like you can finally move on with your life. It's usually more devastating to Christian mothers, but I remind them that we also have hope. We know the Lord will help us work through the misery. You realize that God is still God, and these things have happened and you have come out in a different, higher place. It's like the analogy someone made of climbing up a set of steep steps to heaven and banging your shin on the riser. It hurts, and you stop. Then you climb a couple more steps, and you bang your shin on the riser again. It still hurts—hurts again—but you're up another level."

When mothers confide that they feel a physical aversion to their gay sons, Evelyn assures them this is a normal response. She recommends books to them, especially *Where Does a Mother Go to Resign?* and *Stick a Geranium in Your Hat and Be Happy.* And then she shares other words of wisdom she has collected over the years.

"Rick Godwin preached a sermon that touched my heart. The most encouraging part of the sermon was when he related the Christian walk to the work of athletes. He said to reach the A level of baseball, which he compared with Christian maturity, you have to have A-level coaches. Barbara Johnson has been my A-level coach. I have had a couple of other topnotch Christian coaches, but Barb has been the A-level leader for me. Another thing about being an A-level athlete is that you have to play even when you're hurt. The workouts, no matter how much they hurt, are designed to strengthen you and improve your skills. The line I liked the most in his sermon was this: 'You can throw up, but you can't quit!'"

She also appreciates this wisdom attributed to Chinese evangelist Watchman Nee: "When the day comes for me as it came for Hannah that my Samuel, in whom my hopes are centered, passes out of my hands and into God's, then I shall know what it really means to worship Him. For worship follows in the wake of the cross, where God is all and in all. When our hands are emptied of all we hold dear and the focus shifts from ourselves to God, that is worship."

The old preacher who wrote the book *Bible Jewels* said that the sapphire represents faith in suffering and in serving others.

By the way she lives her life—serving others even as she struggles to hold together her own broken heart—Evelyn Harris is like the sapphire. She is one of God's most precious jewels. And like Charlemagne's magnificent sapphire clasp whose value is eclipsed by that priceless splinter of cross, there is something more cherished than any gemstone, more powerful than any sorrow, in Evelyn's life today: her unwavering faith in Jesus Christ.

Laughing Through the Tears

Evelyn was one of the earliest participants in and supporters of Spatula Ministries, so I know she would love this cartoon:

Reprinted with special permission of King Features Syndicate.

Church bulletin item:
 The Magic of Lassie, a film for the whole family, will be shown Sunday at 5 P.M. in the church hall. Free puppies will be given to all children not accompanied by parents.[3]

The best time to plant a tree was twenty years ago.
The second best time is now.[4]

A woman rushed into the supermarket to pick up a few items. She headed for the express line where the clerk was talking on the phone with his back turned to her. "Excuse me," she said. "I'm in a hurry. Could you check me out, please?"

The clerk turned, stared at her for a second, looked her up and down, smiled, and said, "Not bad!"[5]

The world is a mirror that reflects our own faces. Frown at it, and it shows you a sourpuss. Laugh at it, and it will be your jolly friend.[6]

A good way to judge people is by observing how they treat those who can do them absolutely no good.

Believe your beliefs,
and doubt your doubts.

Because of Good Friday, we can look back and not be afraid.
Because of Easter, we can look ahead and not be afraid.
Because of Ascension Day, we can look up and not be afraid.
Because of Pentecost, we can look inward and not be afraid.[7]

I was counting my blessings . . .
And there you were!

Reprinted with special permission of King Features Syndicate.

The LORD comforts his people and will have pity on those who suffer. (Isaiah 49:13 NCV)

At the End, a New Beginning

Pam's gem: *While you're going through the sludge it's hard to see the other side. . . . I know how my own faith wavered when I was going through the hard times, but through this experience God has taught me to trust Him to take care of the things I just couldn't handle myself. Now it's so rewarding to help someone else climb out of that hole—what Barb calls the cesspool—and achieve a meaningful, rewarding life.*

Pamela Wilson's story begins with a surprise ending. It begins with the day, after thirty-one years of marriage, when her husband walked in from his work commute and said, "I'd like a divorce."

Pam is a beautiful, petite woman with an impish smile. The word *pixie* comes to mind when friends think of her. She has an appealing, all-American nature that reminds us of one of those little Campbell's Soup characters. Today she's such a perky dynamo, it's hard to imagine that she's been through a divorce that left her life in shambles. But she has.

"I was stunned, heartbroken, devastated, and confused. And I didn't even understand at that time that I could fight the divorce," she said. "I was taught total submission. Women's needs and issues were irrelevant. Hearing from childhood and throughout marriage that my thoughts, feelings, and ideas were somehow erroneous certainly contributed to my sense of unworthiness. My role in life was to please my husband, raise my children, and keep house, always with a smile on my face, no matter what. And for thirty-one years, that's what I did."

But suddenly her marriage was over.

"I thought I should be happy because I was doing what I was biblically supposed to do. But the truth was, we had drifted from the church. And I was faking being the constantly happy person. As a result, over the years I had learned not to trust my feelings," she said.

No One to Confide In

Pam's husband had a military career, and they moved their four children sixteen times. "When he would come home and announce another move, I would smile and say, 'Oh, that's . . . really nice,'" Pam said. "And because I thought it was wrong for me to complain about moving and express sadness about leaving my friends behind, I hid those feelings and kept that smile plastered on my face."

As a result of all the moves, when her husband demanded the divorce, Pam had no close friend to confide in. Except for her two high-school children still at home, she felt alone and isolated. She and her husband were seven months into the separation before she even thought to ask him if there was another woman. "We were both from Christian backgrounds, so I didn't even ask for a long time. With my background, I just knew that if he wasn't happy, it was my fault. I had failed. But after seven months, I did ask, and he said, 'Well, she's just a good friend.'" Later she learned there had been other affairs over the years.

As each day passed, Pam felt herself sinking into a dark,

painful vacuum, overwhelmed by shame. It may be hard to understand now, when divorce seems so common. But not too long ago in some areas, divorce was considered a scandalizing failure that branded the left-behind spouse as a wayward pariah, especially within the church. Knowing her parents' strictly legalistic beliefs, Pam was afraid to tell them. "In fact, I *didn't* tell them at all during our first year of separation," she said.

It seems unimaginable to most of us to think that loving parents wouldn't reach out to an adult daughter who had been betrayed and abandoned by her husband. But when Pam, desperately needing their support, finally summoned the courage to tell her parents, they totally rejected her. "They didn't speak to me for two years," she said. "I was devastated by my parents' rejection. It seemed that I never understood how I had constantly tried to please them without receiving any affirmation or acceptance. I suppose I learned this need to please my husband and children from them. I was so demoralized, so ashamed to say the D word, I just felt lost. I backed off even further from the church, backed off from everything and everyone. It was a *very* difficult time."

Looking back, Pam now sees earlier signs that her marriage had been falling apart—but she couldn't see them then. She held a college degree and over the years had worked sporadically as a teacher, but mostly she had devoted herself to her husband and their four children. As her husband neared military retirement, she had realized she needed to prepare for a life after all the children left home. "I was feeling desperate, knowing my kids would be gone and my husband was always traveling with the military and would continue traveling in his job after the military retirement. I needed some kind of enrichment—a job—and my kids and husband said they had no problem with that."

So she had enrolled in graduate school, taking night classes in psychology for three years to complete her master's degree. She would get up each day around 6 A.M. to see the kids off to school and get her housework and her homework done. She prepared dinner so that her kids and husband, when he was home, would have a home-cooked meal each night. Then she headed off to campus for her classes, returning home about 11 P.M. to sleep a few hours and do it all over again.

When her husband left the military, he accepted a job several hours' drive away. He and Pam had decided that she and the kids would stay put so that she could complete her studies and set up her practice as a licensed therapist and the two younger kids could finish out their high-school years without having to move again. "My husband and kids said they had no problem with what I was doing. Looking back, though, I see the enormous pain and the split in myself—trying to hold it all together but on the inside feeling so insecure and shaky. Even though I wouldn't admit it then, I was really unhappy for a long time—and he was too. What brought me true joy was my children. They seemed to fill in the gaps."

"The Kids Just Fell Apart"

Tragically, when the four children were told their parents were getting divorced, they turned on Pam, blaming her because she hadn't dropped her career plans, pulled the younger ones out of school, and followed her husband to yet another city. "The kids just fell apart," Pam said. "Now I know there's no reason to believe young adults can accept their parents' divorce any better than younger kids. My kids were so angry with both my husband and me, we would lose them for weeks at a time when they wouldn't speak to either of us. The ones at home would rage at me, and then I'd get angry, abusive phone calls from my older kids in college." She didn't tell them about their father's affair.

Her loved ones' reaction reinforced Pam's feelings of failure. And those feelings were amplified as she helplessly watched one of her adult sons bury himself in drugs and promiscuous sex. Pam wondered how her life had become so tormented. Inwardly, she felt hurt and angry about what was happening to her and her family. "But somehow there was a part of me that felt I deserved it all or that I had caused it all because I had not done as my parents had pushed me all my life to do—be the dutiful wife." She felt as though she were drowning in the sea of shame.

Ironically, even with her fresh background in psychology, it took awhile for Pam to realize her own need for help. But when she did, "it was such a relief to go in and spill everything in the therapist's office. My parents had totally rejected me. My kids were mad at me. I had failed to make my husband happy, and he had left me. Everything seemed hopeless. The therapist got me to dig out my anger at their responses—to say yes, I *was* mad. And then she helped me work through that anger and reach the forgiveness phase."

Then it was finished. The divorce was finalized.

A month later—on Pam's birthday—her ex-husband came to tell her he was getting married.

By then her children were out of the home, and Pam was struggling to reestablish a life for herself. "We had to sell our home, of course, and I moved into a small condo. During thirty-one years of marriage, I'd never even balanced the checkbook, and for the first time in my life, I had to open a bank account in only my name, get checks printed with only my name, arrange for utilities to be turned on, and get insurance in only my own name. And I had to fight for a credit rating. I was fifty-two years old before I had a credit card in my own name," she said. And after thirty-one years of a middle-class lifestyle, she found out what it was like to be poor. Now she laughs when she looks back on those days. "I don't think I bought a pair of shoes or a piece of clothing for four years."

A Sense of Peace and Accomplishment

As Pam slowly but determinedly began her new life, she also worked to build up her counseling practice. And it was there that she turned misery into ministry. In the years since her divorce she has found a sense of peace and accomplishment that propels her to reach out to others who are treading that rocky ground she once stumbled over. Having experienced the enormous relief from letting go of the anger toward her parents, Pam went through the same process and was able to forgive her children for their judgment. Finally, and perhaps most amazingly, she learned to be friends with her ex-husband and his new wife, knowing there would be many family events in the future—weddings and grandbabies' births—when they would find themselves in the same room. She realized by forgiving him she accepted responsibility for her part in the events that led up to the divorce. She was determined that what had happened in the past would not spoil those joyful events for her children and their families, and she has kept that vow and maintained a civil relationship with this man toward whom she could justifiably show nothing but contempt.

Then, after two years of being shunned by her parents, she dropped her mother and father a note. It simply told them that she had missed communicating with them about what the kids were doing. Immediately her parents called her back, and the relationship—although not as close as it once had appeared to be—has been restored. "They continue to blame me for the divorce," Pam said, "but I've learned how to respond and not take in their attitude."

There have been some lonely and painful times for Pam since the divorce. But there has been bountiful joy, as well. "As angry and hurt as I was at my kids, there have been some awfully good times in all this, too," she said. "Sometimes my drug-dealing son would talk to me about what he was going through, and I would listen, pray, and give him a safe place to talk and feel. I couldn't 'cure him,' but I continued to confirm my love for him and encouraged him to return to a relationship with the Lord. I kept repeating those sentiments while it seemed he was falling further and further away. But he finally got his life turned around, and today—of all things—he's a *minister!*"

Now she says, "Having gone through my own therapy equipped me with the necessary tools to be a far better parent and to experience a more meaningful relationship with my children."

Happy On Her Own

Pam has turned her life around. "One day as I was standing alone in the condo after my youngest child had left home, I suddenly relished the fact that I felt *good* about my life. I felt a sense of purpose—helping others—and my life no longer revolved around my children. I was fulfilled and happy on my own. I didn't depend on someone else for my happiness."

That's not to say she isn't completely giddy over her grandchildren. But she can enjoy being with them without being devastated when they and their parents have to leave. Pam now has a career that makes her feel valued and trusted. "I love what I do," she said. "I expect to be a licensed therapist forever—until I can't remember people's names when they walk in the door. I love watching people change and grow . . . from resistance and shame into feeling better about themselves. It's one of the most emotionally rewarding careers I could ever imagine."

Many of Pam's clients are women much like she was a few years ago. Pam tells them, "I know that while you're going through the sludge it's hard to see the other side. Sometimes you just think, *I'd be better off dead—everyone would be better off if I were dead.* But think of your kids. You wouldn't want to do that to them after what they've been through. When you're tottering on the brink, it's hard to believe you'll be okay and your kids will be okay—that you will survive. I know how my own faith wavered when I was going through the hard times, but through this experience God has taught me to trust Him to take care of the things I just couldn't handle myself. Now it's so rewarding to help someone else climb out of that hole—what Barb calls the cesspool—and achieve a meaningful, rewarding life."

"Divorce Is Not an Option!"

Today both men and women come to Pam seeking help in restoring their marriages. She urges them to stay in close communication and always, no matter how painful it is, to work out their differences. Recently when a couple arrived in her office, looking for help in restoring their marriage, Pam began by telling them, "In this case, where you seem to have simply 'fallen out of love,' let's agree: Divorce is not an option!"

Pam acknowledges that there are situations—abuse and infidelity, for instance—where divorce *is* an option. She often works with women who remind her so painfully of herself a few years ago: women whose husbands have left them and who now feel helpless and hopeless about the future. Gently but firmly, Pam guides them through recovery until they've reclaimed their self-esteem and found ways to restore God-filled meaning and purpose in their lives in their own right, apart from their families. She tells clients, "You won't need therapy forever. What therapy will do is give you the tools you can use yourself to keep your life on track."

She also knows there are many hurting women out there in bitter, empty marriages who cannot or will not seek therapy. "Many times, the woman doesn't seek help because her husband discourages it or she comes from a background where having a therapist is a sign of weakness," she said. "What should be stressed is that there is absolutely no shame in needing help. None of us has all the answers, and sometimes we need someone else to come alongside us and encourage us. But if a woman can't go to a therapist, I hope she'll look at some good Christian psychology books and also some good Christian videos on marriage and communication. My advice is to seek out help from Christian professionals and writers. Those professionals who aren't believers often encourage clients to divorce too quickly. They say, 'If it doesn't feel right, then get out and move on.' That's very poor advice. Many of those marriages are worth saving. But it takes both spouses working at it."

Out of Pain, a Pearl

Pam's work is her ministry, and it perfectly epitomizes a beautiful pearl with its soft, warm glow. Unlike the other jewels described in this book, the pearl comes from a living creature. A grain of sand or a minuscule piece of grit, something irritating and perhaps painful, is introduced either accidentally or deliberately inside the shell of a mollusk. And in response to the distressing sensation, the creature secretes a substance called *nacre* that gradually builds up, layer by layer, over the tiny irritant, numbing it, until it is totally and thickly encased in what we call a pearl. It's impossible to tell from looking at the outside of a mussel or oyster whether there's a pearl inside. Only when the shellfish is broken apart is the pearl revealed in the dying mollusk.

Like the almost indiscernible growth of the nacre inside the oyster, Pam's unhappiness grew almost imperceptibly in a long, seemingly healthy relationship where her value went unrecognized. Now, when she looks back on those years, she sees how God was preparing her for what was ahead. When her marriage broke apart, it felt like a death to her. But slowly she realized that something good could come of her distress. And today, when she helps another humiliated, distraught person grow into a purpose-filled life after a devastating emotional blow, she knows exactly what that "something good" is.

In Jesus' day, pearls, not diamonds, were the jewels of greatest value, and in Matthew 13, Jesus told a parable comparing Himself to a "pearl of great price." Indeed, He is worth *everything* to us. As the writer of the little book *Bible Jewels* noted more than a century ago, "If you are sick or in pain or if in sorrow for the death of your father, or mother, or some dear friend, it won't take away your pain or help you to bear it or comfort you in any way to have a string of pearls tied round your neck. A common pearl can't give any comfort then. But Jesus, the 'Pearl of great price,' can. He says in the Bible, 'As one whom his mother comforteth, so will I comfort you' [Isaiah 66:13 KJV]. What a sweet promise that is! Nobody can comfort like a mother. . . . But . . . Jesus can; yes, and better even than any mother."[1]

When I think of Pam's story, I think of a pearl, because out of something painful and broken in her own life, Pam has created a ministry of work that brings Christ-centered comfort and encouragement to those in distress.

Laughing Through the Tears

One of the ways Pam brings comfort is to help her clients use humor as a tool. It is, she says, a necessity in surviving hard times. Here's some of the funny stuff she and I have shared.

Each of us has a string of pearls in our hearts. These "pearls" are the beautiful moments we've experienced in our lives, moments that become memories and will *uplift, enliven, gladden, soften, inspire,* and *guide* us. There are plenty of baubles, bangles, and beads in life, but only a few gems. Close your eyes and see your string of pearls. Name the gems by name, by place, by experiences, by gifts of the spirit. Whether or not you wear jewelry, always wear your spiritual string of pearls!

—CATHY FESTE

"O.K., Sweeties. You're all going to need to go naked for just a day or two till Mommy catches up with the laundry."

You gain strength, courage, and confidence by every experience in which you really stop to look fear in the face. You are able to say to yourself, "I lived through this horror. I can take the next thing that comes along." You must do the thing you think you cannot do.

—ELEANOR ROOSEVELT

ZIGGY   **By Tom Wilson**

A man walked into a dentist's office and asked the charge for extracting wisdom teeth. "Eighty dollars," the dentist said.

"That's ridiculous!" the man said. "Isn't there a cheaper way?"

"Well," the dentist mused, "if we don't use anesthetic, I can knock it down to sixty dollars."

"Still too much," the man answered.

"Okay," said the dentist, "if I save on anesthesia and simply rip the teeth out with a pair of pliers, I could get away with charging twenty dollars."

"Still too much," the man moaned.

"Hmmm," the dentist said, scratching his head. "If I let one of my students do it for the experience, I suppose I could charge you just ten dollars."

"Marvelous!" said the man. "Book my wife for next Tuesday."[2]

Doctor to patient: "By the way, do you still have those pills I gave you last week? They were beads my wife wanted to have restrung."

A woman was dying. A priest was summoned, and he attempted to comfort her, but to no avail.

"I am lost," she said. "I have ruined my life and every life around me. Now I'm going painfully to hell. There is no hope for me."

The priest saw a framed picture of a pretty girl on the dresser. "Who is this?" he asked. The woman brightened. "She's my daughter, the one beautiful thing in my life."

"And would you help her if she were in trouble or made a mistake? Would you forgive her? Would you still love her?"

"Of course I would!" cried the woman. "I would do anything for her! Why do you ask such a question?"

"Because I want you to know," said the priest, "that God has a picture of you on His dresser."[3]

I give them eternal life, and they shall never perish; no one can snatch them out of my hand. (John 10:28)

Reaching Out
from Death's Doorway

Rose's gem: *I say, "Lord, I don't know the words You want me to say. I don't know how to approach this. You're going to have to do it for me. Give me wisdom from the Holy Spirit." And then I approach each person with confidence, knowing He is with me.*

ose and Glenn Allen were a vibrant couple, full of energy and fun, and they enjoyed doing things together. Both of them had been blessed with excellent health and great joy, and they seemed to be living the "happily ever after" part of a storybook life.

They had met when she was working for Sears & Roebuck and he was an electrician with his own company. One of his employees matched them up, and the first time he saw Rose, her hair was set in curlers—not exactly the first impression she had planned. "We were friends for a year," she said, "and then he went into the service. I wrote him letters and signed them, 'Your friend, Rose.' He wrote back and said, 'Could you

sign your letters a different way?' After that I ended each letter with 'Love.' He was a wonderful guy."

They were married in 1954, and their only child, a daughter, was born a few years later. Rose and Glenn had a good life
together over the next thirty-seven years. They had the kind
of marriage that made them best friends as well as husband
and wife, and they cherished their time together.

Lessons Learned in Heartache

"Over the years, Glenn taught me fishing, and I taught him
about the art world and, most importantly, about Jesus," Rose
said. "What more could I want?"

In their later years, one of the ways they stayed in shape
was to walk together every morning. Their walking routine
often served as a warmup for Glenn before he headed off to
play golf. He was a very athletic man, and he played the
game with great enthusiasm. One summer, however, Glenn
developed a lingering cough that hung on despite throat
lozenges and cough syrups. When he and Rose walked, she
walked faster than he did, and he quickly became short of
breath.

It took a lot of persuading to get him to go to the doctor, but
Glenn finally agreed. During the exam, the doctor pronounced
him in perfect health—except for one little thing: an elevated
white cell count. "Most doctors would probably have given
him some antibiotic, sent him home, and told him to come
back in two weeks," said Rose. "But this doctor dug a little
more. He wanted to know what was causing the problem, and
after some tests he finally decided it was something in the
lung but he didn't know what."

Exploratory surgery was scheduled. That day, Rose nervously waited in the hospital lobby with two close friends,
and when the surgeon came to talk to her he brought two
other doctors with him. Rose watched the doctors' grim faces
and knew her happy life was about to change.

Glenn had cancer—extensive, inoperable, terminal cancer.

He lived six months. And now, looking back, Rose sees the

extraordinary learning experience God provided her in those agonizing, trying days.

Glenn came home from the hospital after the surgery but returned for two difficult courses of chemotherapy. Nothing slowed the ravaging cancer. But at the same time, nothing hindered his or Rose's faith.

Rose had grown up in a loving home on Long Island, New York, but her parents weren't regular churchgoers. "They were Easter Christians," she said. "Some Sundays I would go by myself to the little community church, but I didn't go often." In a few years, the family moved to California, and Rose became friends with a girl from a Christian home. "I went to church with her and enjoyed it. But I didn't go all the time, and really, the main reason I attended was to see the boys who were there."

When Rose was fourteen, her father died suddenly and unexpectedly. She and her mother were devastated. "I was an only child, and I had idolized my father as young girls do. This was the only death I'd ever known except for losing pets, and it took me a long time to get over it."

But as often happens, the difficult experience pushed Rose closer to God, and within a year of her father's death, she was baptized. When she and Glenn married, he was not a Christian, and she drifted away from the church. They were "Easter Christians," as her parents had been. Then, when their daughter, Terri, was four years old, "she started asking simple little questions, and I realized I needed to get back into the church, both for my daughter and for myself," Rose said.

She and Terri began attending Sunday school, and Rose became enthralled by the teaching of the woman who led her class. "I would rush home and do my homework in the old-style Standard Publishing workbook. Working through it, I'd say to Glenn, 'Did you know this: . . . ?' He'd say, 'No, I don't believe that.' And we'd sit there and spend hours going over the Word—not arguing but conversing and learning. Before you knew it, Glenn was coming to church with us."

Eventually Glenn became a deacon and then an elder in the

church, and Rose served as a Sunday school teacher and then as Sunday school superintendent. Later she worked at several other churches as director of Christian education. "Glenn was a quiet man, and for him to stand up and do meditations was difficult for him. But he became very good at it. I had no background at all in teaching, but the Lord blessed me mightily. Over the years I did Christian education for all ages, from two- and three-year-olds to senior citizens, and I developed programs and loved every bit of it."

Next came a time when Rose wanted to look for a part-time job. She started out at a nearby Christian bookstore, where one of the regular customers was . . . Barbara Johnson! She and I became friends, and our friendship continued when Rose left the bookstore to become a Christian education consultant for Standard Publishing. She was working there when her mother passed away and a year after that, when Glenn was diagnosed with cancer.

"As traumatic as his illness was, it was an experience I learned from," Rose said. "I learned from Glenn. For example, there was a time when he was home and in a wheelchair, and someone came to visit and asked him if he was angry at God. After all, Glenn was only fifty-nine; that's awfully young to have terminal cancer. Glenn looked really shocked by the question. His eyebrows went up and his eyes got big. He said, 'Oh, no! Not at all. God didn't give me this cancer. This is what *life* dealt me. But it's God who'll see me through it.'"

"How *Can* You, God?"

It took awhile for Rose to learn that lesson. "Glenn chose to die in the hospital, because he believed that would be easier for me, and I guess it was," she said. "But one day I was driving home from the hospital, and my eyes filled with tears so quickly that I had to pull off the road. I sat there crying and screaming at God: 'How can You do this? He's such a good guy. How *can* You, God? I don't even know that You're here. Nothing's happening to show me You're at work here, that You're standing with me through this.' I was in such terrible pain, such grief—

the kind David talked about in the psalms, the kind that stirs up guttural sounds in the soul. It scared me to hear myself sobbing that way. And then, after a while, I didn't hear a voice, but something in my mind clicked, and it was as though He said to me, 'I *am* here. You just haven't looked around. Look how your church is helping you, how your friends are supporting you in prayer.' That's when I realized that God is with us in the people who support us—surrounding us and holding us up when we're too weak to stand on our own."

Rose was determined to make the most of Glenn's last days. Sometimes in the hospital she climbed into his hospital bed so they could cuddle as they watched a favorite TV show. "I think during that time we became even closer than we had been before. Sometimes I just couldn't help but touch his arm while he was sleeping. I needed to keep a connection between us," she said.

On one of their last days together, Rose noticed Glenn staring intently at the ceiling. "What are you looking at?" she asked.

"A light," he told her.

"What about the light?" she asked. Being the longtime wife of a master electrician, she was accustomed to having him look at lights and say they hadn't been installed correctly.

"It's so bright!" he said in amazement.

Rose couldn't see that the light was any brighter than any other lights in the hospital. Later, looking back, she would see that beacon as God's way of telling Glenn it was time to go.

Glenn died quietly a few days later when Rose and Terri had slipped away to rest at home for a couple of hours. "We had been there most of the night, and our home was nearby. He was sleeping—in kind of a coma—and we decided to slip home for a little while."

At first Rose was upset with Glenn for dying while she was gone. And her anger would build when, during the days after his death, she would find something at home that needed to be repaired. "I'd think, *Now, why couldn't you have fixed that before you died?*"

A Lifeline Thrown into the Pit

At times, Rose's grief threatened to completely overwhelm her, and she felt herself sliding deeper and deeper into a pit, even as she struggled to keep up a normal appearance to her friends. "I hated it when they said to me, 'You're so strong, Rose,' because I knew what I was like when I got back home. Sometimes I would pray, 'Please, Lord, don't let me break down in front of those people. They get so tired of seeing me weep.' I've learned from my own experience that grieving people sometimes manage to appear to be strong when they have to be, but when they're alone, they're not strong at all."

One of the friends Rose made during that time was a registered nurse who introduced her to a Christian hospice organization. "I know all hospice groups are wonderful—I've been involved with several—but there's a certain difference in the Christian organization."

Rose turned her misery into ministry when she joined the Christian hospice as a volunteer serving bereaved families. She has served the organization selflessly ever since. Today she not only works as a volunteer to hospice families, she also facilitates a bereavement support group for men and women who have lost family and friends.

"It has helped me as much as I hope I've helped the grieving families," she said. "It's been a great thing for me, just as the Scripture says in 2 Corinthians 1:3–5: 'All praise to the God and Father of our Master, Jesus the Messiah! Father of all mercy! God of all healing counsel! He comes alongside us when we go through hard times, and before you know it, he brings us alongside someone else who is going through hard times so that we can be there for that person just as God was there for us' (MSG). Barb quoted a line in one of her books. I underlined the words and folded down the page: 'We are each of us angels with only one wing. We fly only by embracing each other.' When you can *do* for other people, it helps *you* a great deal. I've definitely learned that."

One of the lessons came in the early days of her own grief when Rose forced herself to do something she didn't want to do. "Before Glenn knew he had cancer, there was a young woman in our lives, in her mid-twenties with two kids—and she had cancer. She was our friend, and she thought of Glenn as her dad because hers had died. When Glenn died, she was beside herself—both because he had died and because she wasn't physically able to go to the memorial service. I knew I should go see her afterward. I knew she was hurting. But I wondered if I could really do it. After all, she was suffering the same disease my Glenn had died from, and I just wasn't sure I could go back into that scene and offer any comfort.

"My stomach was in knots about it. I prayed about it, and God seemed to be telling me to go, but I still didn't know if I could. I did *not* want to knock on that door! But finally I did go—and that sweet young gal was such a blessing to *me*. She was in bed in her home, and her attitude was so wonderful. She was very uplifting, and she talked to me about Glenn and how much he had meant to her. When I left her, I felt God had lifted me up through her. And it came to me then: *Rose, you can do this, and it's important that you do.* So now I always try to do things on a one-on-one basis when someone has lost a loved one. Because I've gone through it, I understand," she said.

The Healing Power of Tears

Rose knows that grieving people are expected to "get over it" and return to "normal" in a few weeks or even months. She's learned, though, that grief has its own schedule. "One of the things I do for hospice is to make the three-month follow-up calls. Three months after the death, I call the family and usually say, 'I'm just calling to see how you're doing. Are you okay? How are you dealing with this grief?' Sometimes, they just answer, 'Fine,' and I have to keep going, keep probing a little, very gently. Maybe I ask if they're sleeping okay, or I ask about children or grandchildren. In the phone calls and in my other hospice work through grief support groups, I try to build a relationship with these families. Sometimes I'll ask a spouse or loved one how he or she is doing, and immediately there will be tears. When that happens, I just let the person cry, because I know the healing power of tears. In fact, I think the ones who cry are the easiest ones to help. So I wait, and I say, 'You go ahead and cry, Honey, because that's the way we heal.' And later I tell them, 'Each time you cry you've taken one more step to healing.' As Barb says, 'tears, talking, and time' are the steps that propel us through the grieving process. And of course we add one more: prayer."

When Rose calls the families who have lost loved ones and facilitates grief support groups, the most important gift she gives is the gift of a listening, empathetic heart. "I try to get them to talk, and I just listen," she said. "That helped *me* so much after Glenn died—people who would listen to me talk about him. And my church friends would hug me when I was missing those hugs from Glenn. They would tell me they loved me and that they were praying for me. I didn't want to hear Scripture verses when my grief was so fresh and raw. It felt condescending for someone to tell me Glenn was 'in a better place.' I would think, *I know where he is. I don't want to hear that; it's not helping me.* The ones who helped me most simply listened and held me. They didn't have anything profound to say. They just showed me that they loved me."

Reaching Out in Christlike Love

Showing Christlike love is Rose's goal whenever she makes a hospice call or leads a group. Always, before making a hospice call to the family, Rose spends awhile in prayer. "I say, 'Lord, I don't know the words You want me to say. I don't know how to approach this. You're going to have to do it for me. Give me wisdom from the Holy Spirit.' And then I approach each person with confidence, knowing He is with me. I tell myself, *If He was with Moses as he approached Pharaoh, then He will be with me as well.*"

Rose reaches out to make whatever contact is appropriate—a hug or a handshake. "Right now I have a friend in her eighties who's like a second mother to me—and she's dying. When I visit, I take her hand, because I know how important touch is. I make that contact first, get that physical contact going. Then maybe I ask some leading questions: 'How was your day today?' And I ask her to reminisce: 'How did you meet your husband?' Then I just let her go on wherever she wants to take the conversation. Eventually I may ask, 'Have you made arrangements for something you'd like to be done?' 'Do you want to talk about what you're going through?' They may have some unfinished business, some arrangements they want to have made, and I offer to help with anything I can do. My friend gives me a gift every time I'm there. She always has one humorous thing saved up to tell me. I love that."

Rose also counsels the families who may feel abandoned by friends. "There are people who have been friends for years who won't come to see you when you're terminal. It's just a fact of life. I always say, 'Don't be angry with your friends. They're grieving, too, and some people just can't handle it.'"

Rose has learned the value of a positive attitude. She is one of those gifted learners who eagerly look for life lessons in every minute of every day. Besides being a hospice volunteer and a Christian education expert, she is also an artist who gives away most of her beautiful works to friends. In fact, she gave me a precious drawing like the one on page 145. And she is a grandmother. A few years ago when her daughter was going through a divorce, Rose made a point of focusing on her two grandchildren, Andrea, who was three, and Austin, six. "Austin was having a hard time with it. He used to talk about it a lot, saying things like, 'I don't want this dee-vorce,' as he called it. Then he closed up and didn't say much at all, didn't smile as much. I knew he was going through grief, just like so many of the people I work with. I prayed, *Lord, what can I do to help little Austin?*"

The Magic Note

The idea flowed out of Rose just like all the other good deeds she bestows on others. "I wrote him a little note about all the things I liked about him—things he once had but now didn't have a whole lot of. It was just a note of affirmations:

Dear Austin, today I was thinking about you and decided to tell you why I like you. I really like your smile because it makes me feel good all over. I like how you're interested in many things, the way you draw great pictures (especially when they're for me). I like how you do things for your mom and sister and how you are kind to them and take care of them. I like how you tell the truth and do the right thing. But most of all I like the wonderful hugs and kisses you give me. You make me feel special, but that's because you're a very special boy. You are God's special boy! I love you!

Even though Austin's parents have worked hard to build him up with love and support, Rose's note full of written affirmations seemed to work magic. "Austin read the note. Then he wanted my daughter to read it to him. He insisted she read it five more times. And when his father came to pick him up, Austin had the note read to Daddy. Austin took the note to his dad's house and asked if he could sleep with it under his pillow. Everything that is special to Austin goes with him to bed and gets tucked under his pillow," Rose said. "What a lesson that was to all of us to remind us how powerful our words can be."

The Hidden Beauty of the Agate

The lessons Rose learns increase her value as one of God's most precious jewels. There are so many widows out there who completely fall apart after their husbands die. I see them wither away, so self-absorbed in their grief that they can barely see beyond the end of their noses. Rose could have been one of them. But she deliberately chose to *use* her grief to propel her into a ministry of serving others with broken hearts. She is like the beautiful agate, another one of the jewels designated for the Jewish high priest's "breastplate of judgment" in Exodus 28 and 39.

Agates often occur as "nodular masses." On the outside, these nodules usually resemble nondescript rocks that might otherwise be cast aside. Expert geologists recognize these plain-looking rocks for what they are, but they must break the agates to maximize their potential, because the agate's beauty is found *inside* the lackluster shell of stone. And what spectacular beauty is there: often an astonishing arrangement of rings and crystals in the most beautiful range of colors imaginable. The nineteenth-century writer said the agate is as colorful as Joseph's coat of many colors: "White and yellow, and brown, and red, and black, and green . . . not mingling together, as they do in the opal, but in different lines, or layers, or rings. Sometimes these different colors are seen in a sort of wavy lines that look like ribbons. Sometimes they are in zigzag lines, like the walls of fortification. And sometimes they are in circles, looking just as if different colored rings had been dropped in when the . . . agates . . . [were] in a melted state."[1]

That description is a perfect image of Rose's life. Only when her heart was broken was her true inner value revealed, her vibrant love for Jesus that swirled within her so vividly that it looped out and zigzagged forth and touched the lives of countless others. Especially those in mourning. We think of the colors of grief as black and brown and navy; yet in the agate those colors appear as beautiful rings of color banded in gentle curves against the lighter, more joyful hues so that the overall effect is a breathtaking work of art by God's own hand. Sometimes in the agate these shapes seem to take on the appearance of a face or a profile of someone famous. Similarly, Rose's work with brokenhearted families and spouses paints a living portrait of the Savior. And there's something else about the agate that reminds me of Rose: Agate can be carved. Beautiful vessels—exquisite bowls and plates and chalices—have been created from this amazing stone, and the resulting pieces are not only appealing in appearance, with their graceful colors swirling throughout the vessel, but they're also pleasant to hold and practical to use. That, too, is Rose: She is a beautiful person, a vibrant Christian, and she has allowed God to carve her into an instrument that is being used mightily by the Lord in this ministry of love.

All those years ago, on the day of her husband's memorial service, one of the ways Rose's friends helped her through the day was to share the gift of laughter. Lynda Wigren, a "jewel" you met in another chapter of this book, was one of those who gathered at Rose's home after the service. "There were a lot of people there, eating and talking," Rose said. "But Lynda and my daughter, Terri, and another friend, Tammy, were in there jokingly arguing among themselves about which pie flavor was my favorite—chocolate meringue or chocolate cream. They had been to Marie Callender's and apparently had quite a hard time deciding what kind of pie to buy for me. They finally bought a chocolate cream, and to escape the houseful of people they brought it into my bedroom with forks and plates. We sat in there hiding from the others and gobbled up that pie. And as we ate that pie, we laughed. What an important thing for us to do on that day, to laugh."

Laughing Through the Tears

Today Rose shares laughter whenever she can. And she has the most delightfully contagious laugh! Here are some giggle gems we've enjoyed together:

There was once a great king who owned a beautiful diamond. But there was a problem. The diamond had a flaw—a noticeable scratch. As a result, the otherwise beautiful gem could never be given or worn or admired.

The king sent word through his vast kingdom that great riches and prestige would come to the person who could take away the flaw. Well, they came, the best of jewelers and artists, even magicians, but alas, no one could remove the scratch. The king despaired.

Then one day a young man arrived, somewhat optimistic about his chances for doing what no one else had been able to do. He quietly set to work, and stayed diligently at his task. Then one afternoon, the young man knocked on the king's door. He handed the diamond to the king. Slowly a smile spread across the king's face. "Yes!" he shouted gleefully. The queen and all the court crowded in for a closer look.

The scratch was still there. But the young man had carved a rose around it, using the scratch for a stem!

Isn't that what God does to our lives? He uses our flaws to create in us a beautiful portrait of Himself.[2]

Rose's artful gift to me:

"Barb—you can't outgive God, but you come close."

The Lord won't take you
where His grace can't keep you.

REVEREND FUN   WWW.REVERENDFUN.COM

©COPYRIGHT 2000 GOSPEL FILMS, INC.

HAVING LOST THE RECIPE, DON TRIED TO MAKE AN
ANGEL FOOD CAKE FROM MEMORY.

We are born broken.
God's grace is the glue that makes us whole.

Most people want to serve God, but only in an advisory
capacity.

I pray that you, being rooted and established in love, may have
power, together with all the saints, to grasp how wide and long
and high and deep is the love of Christ, and to know this love
that surpasses knowledge—that you may be filled to the mea-
sure of all the fullness of God. (Ephesians 3:17–19)

From the Pieces of a Broken Life . . . a Stained-Glass Window of God's Beautiful Love

Christine's gem: *If there are people in your life whom God seems to be directing you to, listen up! God has put them there for a reason. I don't know how I would have survived if Barb and the minister and my parents and sister hadn't shown up that day in the hospital cafeteria and said, "We're gonna help you escape."*

just lying there in the case, tourmaline is beautiful. It occurs in many striking colors, even in *combinations* of vibrant colors within a single crystal (one form, pink with a "rind" of green, is called *watermelon* tourmaline). But the beautiful tourmaline's most amazing property is shown when it is heated or squeezed. The gemstone picks up an electrical charge and becomes a "polarized crystalline magnet," drawing lightweight objects to itself![1] What a perfect jewel to describe Christine McCoy's life. Beautiful and always glowing with a delightful combination of vibrant characteristics, she is fun to be with and inspiring to know. And under the pressure of a physical disability and the adversity of a terrifying first marriage, she developed a charge to share a ministry of kindness and peace, gently drawing to herself the weary people God sends her way. Here's her story:

Christine's parents were both doctors, her grandfather was the associate pastor at a thriving mega-church, and she was the eldest of five daughters. She grew up in a loving, supportive family where church played an important role. "I had a terrific family, and I grew up feeling so loved by the Lord and so precious as His daughter," said Christine. As she talks about her background, she emphasizes how she enjoyed her Sunday school lessons, sang in the church choirs, and played an active part in church youth groups. She often forgets to mention the disability that would be incapacitating to many of us. Christine has a severe visual deficit. In fact, she's legally blind.

She was born too soon during an era when premature babies were put in incubators that supplied double the oxygen content that the babies had received in the womb. Babies that survived the incubator almost always had some kind of visual impairment. As a result of being placed in the incubator, Christine lost all the sight in one eye and a good deal of the sight in the other.

Still, she grew up wanting to be a physician, like her parents, who encouraged her in whatever goals she set for herself, no matter how impossible they seemed. "My parents made me feel so confident that I could do whatever I wanted to do. And of course there were some down sides to that. For example, one time I was riding my bike, and I was hit by a car."

When, during her early studies, she finally accepted the fact that she couldn't be a doctor ("I couldn't even see the cells in a microscope," she said), instead of melting into a puddle of despair, she simply shifted her medical goal to something she was intrinsically suited for. She became a physical therapist, earning a bachelor's degree from the University of California at Santa Barbara and a master's at the University of Southern California. While her eyes couldn't see the cells in a microscope, her hands could sense the stiffness in an injured back or the damage done to a torn knee, and over the years she excelled in helping rehabilitate victims of spinal-cord injuries and those patients who were severely disabled.

But her early adult life wasn't peaceful. While she felt loved and valued within her family, her vision deficit made her shy in public. "I had friends," she said, "but I didn't date much, and I felt reticent around boys."

"It Felt So Good to *Have* Someone"

During college, she met George, a grad student. They were both involved in the same Sunday school at the time, and Christine appreciated his attention. On our second date, he told me, 'God has told me you are going to be part of my life.' And I didn't see a problem with that. It felt so good to *have* someone, to be part of a couple." She didn't even feel there was a problem when George seemed to take on narrowly focused religious legalism and eventually told her that her parents "weren't spirit-filled."

Despite her parents' concerns that the relationship wasn't a healthy one, Christine and George were married. And then the difficulties began. George began exhibiting an explosive temper over the most trivial issues. His unrestrained anger confused and terrified Christine, and she grew increasingly bewildered by her husband's actions. Also, there was always a third person in their apartment—George's teenage friend, Will. "Will was from a church family I knew, and he and George were really good friends," she said.

With Will visiting their home regularly, Christine often felt "like a fifth wheel," but the thing that was most upsetting was George's terrible temper tantrums. "I remember one day he got so mad at me—absolutely furious—because I had somehow sliced the cheese the wrong way for his sandwich," Christine said. Then came the day, just a month after the wedding, when she came home from work to find George lying on the floor. "What's wrong?" she asked him fearfully.

"I can't be married to you anymore," he said slowly in a flat, emotionless voice. "I want a divorce."

Now, many years later, Christine has greater insight into the situation that, back then, turned her life upside down. "It just came to me one day: *George is gay.* Now I know that homosexuals who don't want to be homosexual struggle terribly with their emotions. They feel so torn, so pressured to be something they're not, and often that struggle comes out in anger toward themselves and toward others."

A Hellish Situation

"I just thought, *Somehow we'll get through this.* I knew if God loved and forgave me for all my sins, He could also forgive George. I thought we could make it, and George agreed to try. The three of us would go to church together—George, Will, and I—and I was constantly praying for a miracle. George was always so mad, so temperamental. I loved my work, but weekends were a nightmare because George, Will, and I were usually together. I prayed, and I prayed, but nothing seemed to improve. Some people said I wasn't praying enough, and it was a very difficult, frustrating time. But I kept reading and studying God's Word. What I learned from First Peter is that this world is not my home, that all our difficulties here will be for God's glory as He works through us during the hard times. I felt like I was in that situation Peter described when it feels like the devil is prowling about like a lion seeking whom he might devour."

George became increasingly controlling, wanting to know where Christine was at all times. "I was in a hellish situation, but I believed if I could keep my eyes focused on the Lord, I would be happy in eternity, if not here. I kept believing God would take care of me."

After the first eighteen months of marriage, Christine and George, individually, decided they could no longer stand the isolation and agony caused by their inner turmoil. "I finally told my sister I was married to someone who was gay. And we told George's parents about him and Will. His mother was best friends with Will's mother."

Tragically, George's mother died the next day after learning this news.

Christine and George decided to attend a meeting of Love in Action, a Christian group in San Francisco that reached out to homosexuals. Guess who was the guest speaker!

"Barbara had just published her first book, *Where Does a Mother Go to Resign?*, and after she spoke that night we introduced ourselves to her and discovered she just lived about two miles from us. She invited us to her Spatula meetings in the Crystal Cathedral, and George and I went together."

George was trying not to be gay, but he was losing the fight. "Sometimes after we attended joint counseling sessions and support groups with other couples, the gay men and their wives would meet at a local restaurant, and the guys would dance together in the bar," said Christine. "Other times, I'd come home from work and find him at home with another man from the support group, drinking wine."

As George became increasingly controlling—and more intensely angry—Christine had to work harder to slip away from him. And she also had to work hard to cover up where she was going and what she was doing, especially since she could not drive and had to rely on friends or buses. "I wanted to do things with my parents and sisters, but I didn't want them to know too much about George, and I didn't want him to know I was going. I hated being so clandestine, keeping things from him, but by that time he had a total-control mind-set. He wanted to take over everything about me, even my mind."

A Call for Help

Since Christine couldn't drive due to her vision impairment, George had to drive her to her work and her appointments, or she had to ride the bus. One day when they fought as he drove her to a dentist appointment, he got so angry, he stopped the car, pushed her out onto the highway, then drove away. She managed to get inside a nearby donut shop and find a telephone.

"Barb, could you help me?" she asked.

Now, more than twenty years later, Christine and I look back on some of those events that were so heart-wrenching and hurtful at the time, and we manage to share a giggle or two, recalling our elaborate plans and evasive tactics to get her away from George for a few minutes or a few hours at a time. But back then, as we rushed to escape from his latest temper explosion, we were terrified.

Bill and I helped Christine get a great new job at a cancer hospital, where she worked her way up the ladder to become head of the rehabilitation department. Her career was going great, but her life was falling apart. George wanted Christine to quit her job and devote herself totally to him, so he refused to help her get to the hospital each day. As a result she had to put together an elaborate transportation network to get to work on time. She rode a bus, met a carpool, and then walked part way.

During their marriage, George made regular trips to Las Vegas with Will. One night after one of these trips Will called and warned her, "George is on his way home, and he's really drunk." In fact she later learned he had hit someone with his car that night. "I had just had back surgery, and I remember shaking in fear, wondering what kind of rage he would be in when he got home," she said.

Christine's life had become a living hell. Finally she called a minister in whom she and George had confided earlier and asked him for help. "I feel like I'm down in a deep well with slimy walls, and there's no way out," she said. "I hung up and sobbed, 'God, I just can't take it anymore.'"

A few days later, Christine's sister asked to meet her for lunch in the hospital cafeteria. "I walked in and, my gosh! There was my sister, and there was Barb, too! And, unbelievably, there were my mom and dad—the doctors—eating hotdogs! Mom said, 'Christine, we want to help you get out.' For a minute I was mad, and then instantly, I said, 'Yes, let's do it.'"

Christine was whisked across the country to a safe place,

where she remained for three weeks. Her family had arranged for her to take an emergency leave of absence from work. She eventually came back, strengthened for the bitter divorce proceedings to come and ready to start a new life without George.

"It took two years to get over that feeling of brokenness," she said. "I knew I was in a better situation, but I needed help getting over the broken dreams. I was so blessed to have good friends—Barb, Lynda Wigren, and another friend, Andy. Every week we'd go to Marie Callender's and have chicken salad and peach pie and just have fun and hang out. On the outside, my life was returning to normal, but on the inside I had repressed so much fear and hurt, I needed professional help to get over the nightmares about George I was having. But eventually, I realized I was okay again. I realized I stayed in the marriage as long as I had because I needed to know I'd given it my best shot. There came a day when I was thirty years old and suddenly realized, 'Wow! I can live again!'"

Christine got back into the sports and hobbies she had enjoyed before her marriage. She became a marathon runner. She enjoyed entertaining her many friends and often invited them over for home-cooked meals—flawlessly prepared despite her limited sight.

Limited Sight, Unlimited Potential

She has developed amazing techniques for compensating for her disability. When she pours something into a cup or glass, she rests a finger just over the rim so she can sense when the liquid is near the top. She reads with a magnifier and bright light. And she relies strongly on her other senses. For example, the first time we traveled together and were sharing a hotel room, before we checked out the next morning, Christine carefully made the bed and then lightly ran her hands over every inch of the bedspread.

"You know, the maids will strip the bed anyway," I told her. "You don't have to make it so perfectly."

She laughed. "Oh, it's not that. I have to go over everything in the room with my hands to make sure I'm not leaving anything behind."

It was about that time when Christine's misery turned to ministry. She thrived in her work at the cancer hospital, becoming an expert on pediatric oncology and the role physical therapy plays in recovery. She lectured and even wrote a book so that she could share with others what she had learned—quite a feat for someone who sees only about four letters at a time. "The best analogy is that it's like reading a book by looking through a toilet tissue roll," she said with a laugh.

Just as she has learned to compensate for her limited eyesight, she's also learned to move beyond the hurt George inflicted on her. "I would tell someone else who's going through that situation: 'Speak to your spiritual adviser. When you're so sickly involved and held down by an angry controller, you don't see your way clear to get help. And if there are people in your life whom God seems to be directing you to, listen up! God has put them there for a reason.' I don't know how I would have survived if Barb and the minister and my parents and sister hadn't shown up that day in the hospital cafeteria and said, 'We're gonna help you escape.'"

Then, a few years later, Christine met Kent. "We knew each other from carpooling. We hiked together and backpacked and went car camping. Being outdoors is my passion, and he enjoyed all the things I did."

They were married in 1994, and Kent has been a fabulous husband. I'm reminded of that in all the small thoughtful gestures that are obvious in their home. The first time I visited, I was surprised to see there were no curtains over the windows. "Christine needs all the light she can get to help her see," Kent explained to me. "I don't care anything about curtains—and if it helps her see to have the windows uncovered, then I'm for it. I want to do whatever I can to make things better for her."

Time to Minister

A few years ago, Kent and Christine left California and moved to the Northwest, where they now own a bed-and-breakfast. And in that quiet, peaceful place, Christine's ministry continues.

"Up here, we have time for people, time to minister to all kinds of people. It's a daily blessing to me to see who the Lord brings into our lives: people with cancer, strangers from other countries, travelers who are looking for a place where they can rest and recover from the stress of their regular lives, business folks who are looking for something different from the usual hotel. Once some Japanese businesspeople were here for six weeks. And then there are the people who live in our neighborhood—the senior citizens and a ninth-grader friend who dropped out of school and has now gone back. Because this is a business as well as our home, someone is always here, so the neighbors know we're here for them," Christine said. "I've never felt that the vision thing—my limited sight—has been terrible, but it's made me very sensitive and intuitive. I used that extra gift in physical therapy, and I use it now in meeting our guests at the bed-and-breakfast. I seem to be able to sense the weariness they feel. Or if they're cancer patients, I sense the fear or the uncertainty they may be going through. It's a gift, a blessing, and I'm grateful for it."

Christine likes thinking of her home as a refuge for these weary pilgrims. "I think our appeal is that when people come here, they feel they're home. They feel cared for. They may come down and sit on the lawn and just soak up the peacefulness. We've tried to make this place a haven, a place of peace and joy in this fast-paced world. We've held Bible studies here and church meetings, weddings and art shows. We try to make everyone feel welcome."

Gently Reaching Out to Those Who Search

Indeed, like the warmed and tightly held tourmaline, Christine's warm, welcoming hospitality attracts others to this place of tranquillity. Christine doesn't preach the gospel to these guests who parade through her home. She lives it. "We don't really have anything that shows we're overtly Christian; I don't wear it on my sleeve, as they say. But whenever I can,

I gently talk about my faith to the person who seems to be searching."

For a long time, Christine hesitated to share that she'd been married before to a homosexual man. "For so long, when I was married to George, I was constantly afraid—scared that my cooking wasn't good enough, that *I* wasn't good enough. However, through God's grace, I hope my testimony may help others, just as Barbara's testimony has transformed my life."

Think once again of the beautiful tourmaline—the gem of so many beautiful colors—when you hear the way Christine describes her life today. "I feel like a stained-glass window. God has taken the broken pieces of my life, and He is the framing that holds it together. There have been some hard things about my life. I don't have perfect eyesight, and that has limited some opportunities. And I went through several years of fear and hardship, that's true. But there are many *good* things in my life—my family, my precious husband, the life that we share here, and the wonderful people we meet. I think of those good things as the beautiful jewel colors. And when God holds my life together, it becomes one beautiful piece of art."

Laughing Through the Tears

The really happy person is one who can enjoy the scenery, even on a detour.

Faith is trusting what the eye can't see. Eyes see the prowling lion. Faith sees Daniel's angel.

Eyes see storms. Faith sees Noah's rainbow.

Eyes see giants. Faith sees Canaan.

Your eyes see your faults. Your faith sees your Savior.[2]

God may not always come when you call Him, but He's *always* right on time.

—SYDNEY REDOBLE

When asked what is the secret of a long and happy life, the Duchess of Windsor responded, "Fill what's empty, empty what's full, and scratch where it itches."[3]

HAGAR THE HORRIBLE By Chris Browne

Reprinted with special permission of King Features Syndicate.

The opera house was sold out in anticipation of a world-famous singer's performance there. But when the lights dimmed, an announcement brought a groan from the crowd: "Ladies and gentlemen, we apologize for any disappointment this announcement may cause. Our featured singer has suffered a minor accident and will be unable to perform tonight. We hope you will welcome his understudy warmly."

The crowd muttered and sighed, and the opera began. The stand-in artist gave the performance everything he had. Throughout the evening, there had been nothing but an uneasy silence. Even at the end, no one applauded.

Then, from the balcony, the thin voice of a little girl broke the silence. "Daddy," she called out, "I think you were wonderful!"

The crowd broke into thunderous applause.[4]

Enthusiasm is the sparkle in your eyes; it is the swing in your gait, the grip of your hand, the irresistible surge of your will, and your energy to execute your ideas.

—HENRY FORD

"Mrs. Nortman just sent in this fax of a rash that she's got on her stomach."

Anyone who is having troubles should pray. Anyone who is happy should sing praises. (James 5:13 NCV)

I Never Knew You Lived
So Close to the Floor

Sheila's gem: *In my days of trying to be perfect, life had been all about* me. *Now . . . I realized that my life was supposed to be about others.*

the ruby has been cherished since the earliest biblical times, and today there are ruby mines in Myanmar (formerly Burma) that are older than history. Called *sardius* in the Book of Exodus, the ruby was set in the first row of jewels on the "breastplate of judgment" worn by the Jewish high priest. Later the ruby was one of the gemstones commonly known as *carbuncle,* a pimply-sounding word that meant "little coal." In those days, admirers of the ruby said it reflected the light in a way that made it glow like a tiny ember of burning coal.

My little nineteenth-century book of *Bible Jewels* describes three beliefs that were widely held regarding rubies more than a hundred years ago. Long ago people believed rubies could:

1. Cure sorrow.
2. Shine in the darkness.
3. Keep them from harm.

These stories of the beautiful ruby remind me of my friend Sheila Walsh. It's not that she can do those things attributed to rubies by their admirers long ago. But she has been in those places of sorrow and darkness and danger, and she knows the One who can.

During last year's broadcasts of the Olympics in Sydney, Australia, did you happen to notice the beautiful outline of the Opera House, the city's most famous landmark? Sheila Walsh has performed there to a sold-out audience as she has toured the world promoting her many albums of heart-touching, soul-inspiring music. She worked for the British Broadcasting Corporation in London, hosting a program featuring contemporary Christian and traditional black gospel music. For five years she served as Pat Robertson's co-host on the *700 Club*, a weekday talk show on the Christian Broadcasting Network.

Teetering on the Brink

To have seen Sheila back in 1992, when she was on the *700 Club* every weekday and performing concerts for packed-out audiences most weekends, you would probably have thought she was living her dream. And she was. Almost no one knew back then that Sheila's dream had become a nightmare.

She was teetering on the brink of despair, hanging on to her sanity with the thinnest thread of hope. Her most frequent prayer was, "Lord, please hold me. I'm falling into a dark well," and on one of the darkest days she wrote in her journal, "I feel as if I am disappearing a little more every day. . . . I feel so alone."[1] Sheila had not seen it coming, but she was plunging into a pit of clinical depression. One day while interviewing a guest on the *700 Club*, she had a complete memory lapse and couldn't remember who the guest was or what they were discussing. A few days later, she unexpectedly started to cry while conducting another interview.

About that time she received a letter from an unknown viewer. Now she considers that message one of the most precious gifts she's ever received. It said simply, "I do not know what it is that is causing you so much pain, my dear, but I can see it in your eyes. Please get some help. I am praying for you."

Sheila had grown up in Scotland wanting to be a missionary, and her constant prayer was to promise God she would always be faithful. Again and again she told the Father she would never let Him down; she assured Him that He could always count on her.

To prepare for far-flung mission fields, she attended London Bible College, where she and some friends formed a band and began performing Christian music on college campuses in the area. After graduation, she joined Youth For Christ as a musical evangelist. Then came the world tours, the record contracts, the fame, the privileges . . . and the heartache.

She didn't know where the misery came from, only that it enveloped her life. She was engulfed by an overwhelming sense of failure for having let God down. She was proclaiming the gospel daily yet unable to absorb its life-sustaining strength for herself. "I had always thought that if I just tried hard enough, I could make everything all right. But I had failed," she said. Everything was *not* all right, and she felt powerless to pull her life back together.

She saw herself as a hypocrite, thinking, *How can I sit on national television every day and tell people that if they put their trust in Christ, everything will be all right—when things are far from all right with me?* She had spent much of her life measuring who she was by how other people viewed her. Now the rumor mill carried letters and queries from people who questioned her validity. "People wanted to know what was happening to me. How could I explain to people who called from all around the country what I was struggling to understand myself? I thought I was going to drown," she said.

Constantly she carried in her purse the letter from the old lady. *Please get some help.*

Afraid of Being Swept Away

Finally she did just that. One day in 1992 she completed that day's broadcast of the *700 Club* in Virginia Beach and drove, alone, to a psychiatric hospital near Washington, D.C. There she traded her designer clothes, her beautiful jewelry, her makeup, and even her belts, pantyhose, and hair dryer—things she might have used to hang herself—for hospital garb and slippers. She sat there that night, terrified as she remembered her father, who had died in a psychiatric hospital when Sheila was four years old. She asked the nurse for something to help her sleep, but nothing had been prescribed, so the nurse was unable to help. Before she left the room she told Sheila gently, "I'm sorry that you are in so much pain, and it will probably get worse before it gets better; but you are in a safe place."

Things did get worse as Sheila probed her emotional wounds, looking for a cause—and a cure for her deep depression. A turning point came when a doctor asked her, "So, what is the worst thing that could happen to you, Sheila?"

"I am afraid I will be swept away. I know a couple of people who would gladly destroy my life," she answered.

"Sheila, who is your trust in?" he asked her. "Do you feel as if the Lord has left you?"

His question was the turning point, because Sheila realized the answer was a resounding "No!" She had affirmed that belief in a poem she had written the night before:

> *I never knew you lived so close to the floor,*
> *But every time I am bowed down,*
> *Crushed by this weight of grief,*
> *I feel your hand on my head,*
> *Your breath on my cheek,*
> *Your tears on my neck.*
> *You never tell me to pull myself together,*
> *To stem the flow of many years.*
> *You simply stay by my side*
> *For as long as it takes,*
> *So close to the floor.*

Silent Anger

With the counselors' and doctors' help, Sheila began her journey to healing and hope. She identified the fears that had imprisoned her: the fear of intimacy and the fear of disapproval or failure. And she exposed the silent anger that had raged within her for so long. She learned that her anger sprang from her fears, and she was liberated by the concept of "praying her anger." Throughout her life, she had never given herself permission to be angry. Whenever something happened that should have angered her, she shoved those feelings down in the cellar of her being, grinding her teeth, clenching her hands, but saying nothing. In the hospital, to cope with this rush of anger when it swelled up within her, she learned to "take a step back, . . . go into another room by myself, sit at the Shepherd's feet, and . . . tell Him what I am feeling." In doing so she felt the relief of expressing the pent-up rage that had burdened her before she sought help. Now she urges others, "Let's pray our anger out; let's cry our hurt and pain and fear until we have no tears left. Anger needs to be expressed, and it is much better for us to cry it out to God than to machine-gun our friends with it."

She also dug out the roots of the undeserved but totally absorbing feelings of shame that had tormented her.

Anytime the old feelings of failure threatened her recovery, Sheila reminded herself whose she is. She realized that she had been struggling with the human dichotomy all of us must deal with: "We long to be known because we are lonely, and we fear being known because we may then be loneliest of all" if we are known—and rejected, she said. One reason she had led such a lonely life "was to protect myself from the reaction I might get when the darker side of my life took center stage for a while. I protected myself from rejection by showing up only in situations where I could win. That is a very safe but miserable place to live." In contrast, Christ promises His children, "I know it all, and I still love you." As Sheila says, "That is the convicting, convincing, liberating truth that comes from an encounter with Christ: All is known; there is no need to pretend anymore."

Sheila made advances in her treatment, thanks to medication, professional counseling, and group sessions and activities, where she learned "what it meant to be a part of something, rather than being the whole show myself." Even as she advanced, however, there were times when God seemed painfully silent. "When I prayed, I understood what people meant when they said it seemed their prayers went no higher than the bedroom ceiling. Still, I kept praying, and I kept reading the psalms out loud; it was all I knew to do. David had walked this path before me and had experienced the absence of God. His prayer became my prayer. I prayed out my loneliness. I prayed out my fear and anger. I prayed out the agony of being a fragile, flawed human being."

The Cleansing Power of Forgiveness

She also learned the cleansing benefit of forgiving those who had wronged and hurt her—and asking forgiveness of those she had somehow hurt. In fact, as part of her recovery, she made appointments to see those "who felt disappointed or personally wounded by me."

Finally, Sheila's hospitalization neared an end. She was ready to leave the healing place, but she did not know where to go in her recovery. "That evening, with tears running down my cheeks, I prayed a very simple but life-changing prayer: 'Father, I stand before You now with empty hands. Whatever You put in my hands, I will welcome, and whatever You take away, I will gladly let it go.'"

That first step—praying the prayer—was the easy part, she was to learn. *Living* that prayer would prove to be more difficult. She returned to Virginia Beach, still not knowing whether she would continue on the *700 Club* or strike out on other adventures. Eventually, she decided to enroll in seminary after one last appearance on the show. That day, when the lights went up and the cameras came on, she was the guest, rather than the interviewer, and she told her story honestly and without holding back, describing her struggles with depression, her hospitalization, and her ongoing work to combat the illness. In the month following that final appearance, she received more than five thousand letters from viewers who shared their own struggles with Sheila. She laughs now, saying she instantly became the "poster child for depression." It wasn't what she intended. But it was one of the ways God turned her misery into ministry.

Sheila's doctors assured her that as she continued her recovery outside the hospital she would find new friends as long as she continued to be open and vulnerable. And they were right. Traveling the country with the Women of Faith tour and sharing what she's learned in her books and music, she has grown in joy and in insight through her contacts with thousands of women—and men—who have helped her make an important shift in her attitude. "In my days of trying to be perfect," she said, "life had been all about *me*. Now . . . I realized that my life was supposed to be about others."

"Say a Prayer for Me"

In her book *Honestly,* she tells of a casual encounter that reinforced the value of that shift in attitude. She was standing at a counter, preparing to pay for something she'd bought in a mall store, when a woman came over to her.

"I know you must be busy, and I don't want to keep you, but I would be very grateful if you could say a prayer for me if God brings me to your mind," she said. Sheila looked into her eyes and recognized the pained look of someone barely holding herself together. "Do you have time for a cup of coffee?" she asked the woman.

They made their way to a coffee shop, where the woman told her about the devastating accident the week before that had killed the woman's husband and two small children. Sheila described what happened next:

> We sat there for a while holding hands, tears pouring down our cheeks. There was nothing to say, nothing that would make it any better. After a while, she dried her eyes and got up to leave. We embraced, and she looked

deep into my eyes and thanked me. In one sense I didn't "do" anything. I didn't come up with any clever words or magic prayers. We had just sat for a while together, two people who love God, sharing the heartbreak of life and death.

The old Sheila would have prayed for that woman and hurried on, feeling self-satisfied that I had done a good thing. But this time I really *saw* her, and we touched for a moment and left knowing our only hope is the Lord.

"Write It All Down for Me"

Since those days of recovery, Sheila has suffered her own heartbreaking losses—as well as unspeakable joy. Two years after being treated for depression, she married Barry Pfaehler in a storybook wedding put together by her mother-in-law, Eleanor. Within two years of the wedding, their adorable son, Christian, was born, another heaven-sent gift of joy and love. But within those same two years, Barry's mother was diagnosed with terminal cancer. In her book *Stories from the River of Mercy,* Sheila shares the funny and feisty story of her developing relationship with her mother-in-law—as well as the heartbreaking turn of events. "We stood on opposite sides of an invisible, and seemingly insurmountable, wall," she said. "Eleanor and I talked over this wall. At times we reached up to hug. But the wall was always there. Then Eleanor was diagnosed with liver cancer. Finally, by the grace and mercy of God alone, the wall came crashing down. Eleanor and I found ourselves swimming in the river of mercy with our arms around each other, holding each other, willing to give our lives for each other."

Barry, Sheila, and Christian spent as much time with Barry's parents as they could during that last year of Eleanor's life. The family fought to enjoy every moment they could wring from the days left to her. Then, one morning near the end, Sheila was sitting alone at Eleanor's bedside, watching her sleep, counting the seconds between breaths.

"Mom, I want to ask you something," she whispered. She was remembering what the Women of Faith prayer inter- cessor, Lana Bateman, had told her about sharing a loved one's final days. "Many people will walk with you in your living," Lana had said. "Not many will walk with you in your dying."

Remembering Lana's words, Sheila asked her mother-in-law tentatively, "Mom, do you want to talk about when you die?"

She worried that she would "make Eleanor feel as if I were hurrying her out the exit door." Instead, her mother-in-law "received those words as a starving man would greet an offer of bread."

"Help me up, Sheila. . . . Get a piece of paper and a pen. And bring all my jewelry," Eleanor struggled to say.

When Sheila returned with the requested items, Eleanor began her instructions by saying, "Thank you. Thank you for asking. . . . Write it all down for me, will you?"

With tears rolling down her cheeks, Sheila recorded Eleanor's wishes . . . and later made sure they were carried out.

After Eleanor's death, Barry's dad, William, moved to Nashville to live with Barry, Sheila, and Christian. They loved having him with them at home and on the road. They trav- eled the country together—Sheila, Barry, Christian, William, and Christian's nanny—on the Women of Faith tour, where William was an inexhaustible worker at Sheila's book table.

But their time together was short-lived. Last year William died suddenly and unexpectedly of a heart attack. And again Sheila's heart was filled with sorrow. But something the pas- tor had said at Eleanor's funeral—the same thing she had whispered to herself in those dark days in the psychiatric hos- pital—brought comfort to her again as she, Barry, and Christian worked their way through another valley of grief. The pastor chose the text from Romans 14:8 (NKJV): "For if we live, we live to the Lord; and if we die, we die to the Lord. Therefore, whether we live or die, we are the Lord's." His message reminded Sheila of what she had told herself back when feelings of failure, fear, or shame had threatened to sweep over her again as she was climbing toward the light. *Remember whose you are,* she would say. And that same promise was in the pastor's funeral sermon: "Whether we live or whether we die—no matter what happens to us—we are the Lord's. We belong to Him; we are in His care."

A Magnet of Concern and Empathy

Today Sheila has transcended the brokenness of her life to become real and vulnerable, sharing herself and her story to encourage others everywhere she goes. On the Women of Faith tour, I'm often amazed when I see Sheila at her book table, standing on her high, spiked heels in her high-fashion outfits, talking earnestly—and often tearfully—with the woman at the front of a long line of others waiting to chat with her. The women pour out their hearts to Sheila and draw in her love and encouragement. More than any of us on the Women of Faith tour, Sheila connects with these women who are drawn to her like iron shavings pulled toward a magnet. She listens so intently—and not just as a sympathetic ear. Just as she shared a moment of grief with the woman who stopped her in the mall so many years ago, Sheila expresses an attitude of unhurried concern and empathy. She learns from what she hears and often incorporates her new friends' words and wisdom into the talks she shares so poignantly and dramatically on the stage. And when she does, that new friend feels understood and encouraged by the way God has used *her* in Sheila's message.

It is this part of Sheila's ministry—her vulnerability and her caring concern for others—that shows her true heart. She could be just another recording artist who blows into town, sings her songs, autographs her CDs, poses for pictures, and then scurries back home without connecting to her audience in any way. She *could* do that. But she doesn't. There have been times late on Friday nights after the program is over that I've tried to shoo away the line in front of Sheila's book table, insisting that the women let her get to the hotel and get some rest! She laughs good-naturedly and turns back to the woman in front of her.

Sparkling in God's Light

Sheila is like a ruby—a tough gem, second only to the diamond in hardness but also vulnerable. Because of the way its crystals sometime "twin," it is easily fractured—just as Sheila was. A ruby is beautiful because of its clarity and color and the way it is cut by the jeweler, causing it to reflect and refract the light in a unique way. But away from the light, that's another story. When you stand in the darkness holding a ruby in one hand and an identical-size morsel of coal in the other, you cannot tell which is the precious jewel and which is the chunk of coal. The ruby only sparkles when the light is bright.

A hundred and fifty years ago, admirers collected rubies because they thought they held magical powers—that they could cure sorrow, shine in the darkness, and deliver its wearer from harm. Today we know rubies cannot do any of those things; but the God who created them can. Like a beautiful ruby, Sheila's life sparkles because she stands in God's light, reflecting and scattering it everywhere and sharing God's promise to change sorrow to joy, darkness to hope, and fear to faith.

Back in the late 1800s, the ruby was the "first mineral to be produced by commercial gem synthesis," according to one gem expert.[2] In other words, the first fake jewels were rubies! While those imitations were beautiful, they had no real value, because they were fakes. As a result, many heirs over the generations have brought family treasures for appraisals only to be told that their ruby is not a real gem at all.[3]

For a long time, Sheila felt she was living a fake life. She was proclaiming the gospel to others without claiming its life-saving power in her own struggles. She was a believer and had all the characteristics of a child of God. But she wasn't vulnerable and broken . . . until God shattered her life and put the pieces back together again to create one of His most precious jewels.

Laughing Through the Tears

"Well, what if we held you up to the stove?"

A young mother was sick in bed when her nine-year-old daughter walked in from school. Thinking her mother was asleep, she quietly unfolded the blanket at the foot of the bed and gently tucked it around her mom. The mother stirred, then whispered, "It wasn't too long ago that I was tucking you in. And now you're covering me."

The little girl, bending over her mother, whispered, "We take turns."[4]

A good marriage is the union of two forgivers.

—RUTH BELL GRAHAM

A young couple walked into a bridal shop and asked to see a bridal gown and headpiece. The young woman obviously loved one particular gown and the salesperson suggested that she try it on. Moments later she emerged from a dressing room and stood, a radiant figure in white, in front of her companion. He gazed at her in adoration.

"Would you like to take it?" the salesperson asked.

"Oh, I wish I could, but we can't afford it," said the young woman. "I just wanted my husband to see me dressed the way I might have been. We were married a half hour ago."[5]

DENNIS THE MENACE

"TIME TO GET UP. THIS GUY WANTS TO SEE THE LADY OF THE HOUSE."

God knows the rhythm of my spirit and knows my heart thoughts. He is as close as breathing.[6]

Leo Tolstoy, the great Russian writer, told of the time he was walking down the street and passed a beggar. Tolstoy reached into his pocket to give the beggar some money, but his pocket was empty. Tolstoy turned to the man and said, "I'm sorry, my brother, but I have nothing to give."

The beggar brightened and said, "You have given me more than I asked for—you have called me brother."

To the loved, a word of affection is a morsel, but to the love-starved, a word of affection can be a feast.[7]

"One of us will have to change it, Sylvia, and one of us with my bad back will have to hold the umbrella."

Never will I leave you; never will I forsake you. (Hebrews 13:2)

Like the Stars of the Morning

Barb's gem: *We talk about grief and hardship as time spent in the "the valley." But later, looking back from the hilltop, we see that it was there, in that valley, that we became better persons, selfless servants, stronger Christians. As my daughter-in-love, Shannon, says, we grow when we're down in the valley, because that's where the fertilizer is!*

We have two choices when we're faced with suffering and tragedy. One is to withdraw from life, become bitter, and die inwardly. The other is to reach out to God in whatever way we can and allow Him to use our sorrow for good. When we welcome God's healing presence into our broken lives, we're soon amazed to find His spirit propelling us to reach out to others who are hurting, offering encouragement wherever we find sorrow. Before too long, we realize that true happiness comes by helping others and knowing we are appreciated, even if all we've done is make ourselves available to care and to listen.

In the depths of our misery, we might not have thought ourselves capable of such a turnaround. We might never have pictured ourselves doing the thoughtful deeds we find ourselves doing. And yet there we are, turning misery into ministry.

By sacrificing our energy on behalf of others, we discover there is a priceless reward for those who devote their lives to God's service. Every word spoken to the sorrowful, every act committed to relieve the oppressed, every kindness shown to the brokenhearted will result in blessings, not only to the sufferer, but also to the giver. I love to call this phenomenon "boomerang blessings."

We are refreshed by encouragement when we know others have benefited from our efforts. We are blessed with a warm satisfaction when we allow ourselves to be used in God's service. As He uses us, He transforms our lives in the same way He changes a piece of coal into a diamond. Our tears crystallize into sparkling jewels of blessing that sparkle in the night of despair "like the stars of the morning," shining out in the darkness with the light of God's embracing, sustaining love.

Acknowledgments

many thanks to the twelve women whose stories are shared in this book. How blessed I've been to know them! Their stories have inspired and encouraged me, and I hope their faith, love, courage, and insight have touched your heart as they touched mine. Their willingness to share their painful but powerful transitions from misery to ministry is given as a gift to you and to all who need an uplifting word or a sympathetic ear.

Thanks also to the many friends who sent cartoons, clippings, jokes, quips, and quotes included in the "Laughing Through the Tears" sections at the end of each chapter. In addition, many of these little gems were borrowed from excellent compilations, including: Robert J. Morgan's *Nelson's Complete Book of Stories, Illustrations, and Quotes* (Thomas Nelson, 2000); Lowell D. Strieker's *Nelson's Big Book of Laughter* (Thomas Nelson, 2000); *Draper's Book of Quotations for the Christian World* (Tyndale, 1999); Arthur F. Lenehan's *The Best of Bits & Pieces* (Economics Press, 1994); and Rob Gilbert's *More of the Best of Bits & Pieces* (Economics Press, 1997).

Information about gemstones came from several sources, but particularly from Cally Hall's *Gem Stones*, an Eyewitness Handbook volume published by DK Publishing (1994), and a fragile little volume called *Bible Jewels*, written by the Reverend Richard Newton and published by Robert Carter & Brothers in 1867! I'm also grateful to the kind folks at

Borsheim's, the fabulous jewelry store in Omaha, Nebraska, for sharing informational literature about gemstones.

As always, a host of witty artists and cartoonists have allowed their work to be included here. Thanks to Rose Allen, Dennis Hengeveld, Bunny Hoest, Bil Keane, John McPherson, and Rafael Chacon for personally granting me permission to reprint their cartoons. Other permissions have been granted by the following sources:

Mary Chambers's cartoons are taken from *Motherhood Is Stranger Than Fiction* by Mary Chambers. © 1995 Mary Chambers. Used with permission from InterVarsity Press, P.O. Box 1400, Downers Grove, IL 60515.

Dennis the Menace® used by permission of Hank Ketcham and © by North America Syndicate.

"Reverend Fun" by Dennis Hengeveld is copyrighted by Gospel International Communications, Box 455, Muskegon, MI 49448. Used with permission.

"Bizarro" by Don Piraro, "Non Sequitur" by Wiley Miller, and "Ziggy" cartoons are used with permission of Universal Press Syndicate.

"Hagar the Horrible" by Chris Browne, "Ralph" by Wayne Stayskal, and "Six Chix" by Isabella Bannerman, Margaret Shulock, Rina Piccolo, Ann C. Telnaes, Kathryn LeMieux, and Stephanie Piro are reprinted with special permission of King Features, Inc.

Finally, thanks to you, the reader, for sharing this inspiring journey with me. With millions of books in print, I work with the constant reminder that I am not alone in my quest for faith and merriment. Thank you for the letters you send me, the cheery messages you leave on my telephone answering machine, and the greetings and affection you extend to me when we meet at my book table during Women of Faith conferences. You are my multivitamins, sent from God!

Notes

Opening the Jewel Box
1. Richard Newton, *Bible Jewels* (New York: Robert Carter & Brothers, 1867), 13–14.
2. Ibid.

Chapter 1. A Hostess in God's Filling Station
1. English proverb, quoted from Arthur F. Lenehan, ed., *The Best of Bits & Pieces* (Fairfield, N.J.: Economics Press, 1994), 168.
2. Source unknown.
3. Rob Gilbert, ed., *More of the Best of Bits & Pieces* (Fairfield, N.J.: Economics Press, 1997), 1.

Chapter 3. Sharing the Wealth of God's Unconditional Love
1. Lowell D. Streiker, *Nelson's Big Book of Laughter* (Nashville: Thomas Nelson, 2000), 5.

Chapter 4. Laughter Bubblin' Up from the Boiler Room
1. Thelma's story as told here has been adapted from her inspiring book, *Bumblebees Fly Anyway: Defying the Odds at Work and Home* (Dubuque, Iowa: Kendall/Hunt, 1996).
2. Newton, *Bible Jewels*, 74.

Chapter 5. A Quiet Missionary in Our Midst
1. Cally Hall, *Gemstones* (New York: DK Publishing, 1994), 140.

Chapter 6. Unspeakable Sorrow . . . Inexhaustible Faith . . . and a Crazy Craving for Laughter

1. *Precious in His Sight* (Bloomington, Minn.: Garborg's, 1997).

Chapter 7. Using That Spiritual Get-Out-of-Guilt-Free Card

1. Sandy's story is drawn from interviews and also from her inspiring book, *Soul Hunger,* published by the Remuda Foundation, Inc., P.O. Box 399, Wickenburg, AZ 85358.

2. Geologist Alain Cheilletz of the Center for Petrographic and Geochemical Research in Nancy, France, quoted in "The Geology of Emeralds," *Discover* magazine, May 1999, 35–36. Much of the following discussion is adapted from this insightful article.

3. Adapted from an unidentified magazine article by Ralph A. Micke, "How Wonderful You Are!" quoting *God's Revivalist and Bible Advocate*, Cincinnati, Ohio.

Chapter 8. Waiting for Another Chance to Say, "I Love You"

1. Newton, *Bible Jewels*, 235.

2. Ibid., 237, 245.

3. Adapted from Streiker, *Nelson's Big Book of Laughter*, 67.

4. Chinese proverb, quoted in Gilbert, *More of the Best of Bits & Pieces*, 5.

5. Streiker, *Nelson's Big Book of Laughter*, 89.

6. Gilbert, *More of the Best of Bits & Pieces*, 15.

7. Warren Wiersbe, quoted in Robert J. Morgan, *Nelson's Complete Book of Stories, Illustrations, and Quotes* (Nashville: Thomas Nelson, 2000), 250–51.

Chapter 9. At the End, a New Beginning

1. Newton, *Bible Jewels*, 64.

2. Adapted from Streiker, *Nelson's Big Book of Laughter*, 123.

3. *The Jokesmith*, quoted in Gilbert, *More of the Best of Bits & Pieces*, 73–74.

Chapter 10. Reaching Out from Death's Doorway

1. Newton, *Bible Jewels*, 289–90.

2. Based on an unidentified clipping with this credit line: "Adapted from Anne Brener, *Mitzah*, 231–232."

Chapter 11. From the Pieces of a Broken Life . . . a Stained-Glass Window of God's Beautiful Love

1. www.gemstones.org.

2. Max Lucado, *When God Whispers Your Name*, quoted in Lucado, *Grace for the Moment* (Nashville: Countryman-Nelson: 2000), 220.

3. Streiker, *Nelson's Big Book of Laughter*, 188.

4. Adapted from Lenehan, *The Best of Bits & Pieces*, 122.

Chapter 12. I Never Knew You Lived So Close to the Floor

1. Sheila's story is adapted with her permission from her insightful books *Honestly* (Grand Rapids: Zondervan, 1996) and *Stories from the River of Mercy* (Grand Rapids: Zondervan, 1999).

2. awesomegems.com/gemfacts.html

3. Ibid.

4. Morgan, *Nelson's Complete Book of Stories, Illustrations, and Quotes*, 262.

5. Lenehan, *The Best of Bits & Pieces*, 124.

6. *Precious in His Sight* (Bloomington, Minn.: Garborg's, 1997).

7. Max Lucado, *He Still Moves Stones*, quoted in Lucado, *Grace for the Moment*, 58.

This book has been enjoyed by and shared with:

_____

_____

_____

_____

_____

_____

_____

_____

_____

_____